IRON SHARPENS IRON

Warren Hardig
International Executive Director
Men For Missions International

- *The MFM Pledge* -

I will do whatever God asks me to do;

I will go wherever God asks me to go;

I will give whatever God asks me to give.

CONTENTS

Dedication

This book is dedicated to Jesus Christ, the One who loved me and gave Himself for me that I might have eternal life, and to the many of God's choice servants who see themselves as common, never seeking nor receiving any acclaim or reward this side of heaven.

Acknowledgements

I want to thank all those who have been so generous with their help and prayers. Were it not for the willingness and hard work of the following people, I could not have completed this book.

Dr. Ed Erny, president of OMS International, for his encouragement and support; Ron Mertens of Men For Missions International, for writing and preparing the book for publication. He has left the message of my heart intact; Wynema Coates, my faithful secretary, for hours of research and proofreading; Betty Mellencamp of Greenwood High School for editing; Eleanor Burr, OMS *Outreach* editor, for final editing; Curt Buller, OMS graphics artist, for cover design; and my patient wife, Velma, who is an enduring resource to me.

Above all, I would like to acknowledge the inspiration provided by our Heavenly Father, without which these writings never would have been undertaken.

Preface

We were in his station wagon on Route 75 headed for Miami when Warren first mentioned the book he felt God wanted him to write. It would be stories--not of professional missionaries, preachers, or polished religious types--but rough-hewn laymen whose lives had been revolutionized by contact with other laymen, men drawn by the Spirit of God (frequently against their own will) into an organization called Men For Missions.

"I feel that God gave me a title for the book," he went on.

"What was it?"

"Iron Sharpens Iron."

Since that day I've thought about that title--*Iron Sharpens Iron*. The more I mull it over, the better I like it. The words say two things to me:

First, iron well symbolizes the subjects of this book. Hard men--tough, like Ron Mertens of the Indiana State Police who had almost daily witnessed the brutal and grizzly side of life, a man who had gathered the debris of broken human bodies along state highways, who had photographed blood-splattered rooms where shotgun blasts had left particles of human brain clinging to the ceilings. Tough, sin-hardened, hard-drinking, foul-mouthed men like Warren himself. Take men like these, put them in the company of other men, also men of iron, but instruments forged on the anvil of God. Then let the sharpening process begin--a process in which iron moves against iron until the blunt-edged, rough-hewn metal of life is transformed into an instrument powerful and effective in the hand of God.

But *Iron Sharpens Iron* is fitting for another reason.

OMS, born of God in 1901, designed and shaped by God--His instrument. But in some respects, OMS was still a dull implement. For the first half century, the Mission remained small as its number of missionaries never exceeded 50. Though godly folk in many churches supported and prayed for the small Mission, her manpower was limited. And plans were hampered at every turn by the lack of financial resources. More than this, OMS had little impact on the total life of the church, particularly its men who characteristically regarded missions as a nice philanthropy that could be adequately cared for by the ladies.

Then, God took men of iron--men like Dwight Ferguson, Stanley Tam, Enloe Wallar, Harry Burr, Dick Capin--and fashioned Men For Missions, the laymen's voice of OMS International. In a short time it was clear that a new dimension had been added to OMS. Thousands of laymen began traveling to mission fields, returning with broken hearts, never to be the same. Iron was sharpening iron. These laymen became God's instrument to change OMS, making it immeasurably sharper and fitter--a better instrument for His glory. And the process goes on to this day. Here is a book that chronicles a sharpening in the lives of ten men. In the reading of these pages, you are liable to find yourself laid on the anvil of God. Iron sharpens iron.

Ed Erny, President
OMS International

Introduction

Men For Missions International is the Laymen's Voice of OMS International, an undenominational faith mission with work in 15 nations. As a movement born of the Holy Spirit in the hearts of laymen, MFMI supports the threefold purpose of OMS, which is evangelism, training of nationals, and church planting. This work is carried out daily around the world, bringing truth to the statement that the sun never sets on OMS/MFM efforts to bring men and women to the saving grace of Jesus Christ.

The Men For Missions logo depicts a group of men, arm in arm, circumscribing the earth while standing at the foot of the Cross. This book has been written to share the genius of MFMI as represented by that logo--one man drawing another into the challenge of world evangelism through his life and testimony.

Our priority is the Lordship of Jesus Christ in each man's life. Our mandate is compassion, pure and simple. The requirement for membership remains the same as on the day Dr. Ferguson first formed Men For Missions in 1954. It consists of three simple, yet very powerful, questions. Will you:

Do whatever God asks;
Go wherever God asks;
Give whatever God asks?

The title of this book, *Iron Sharpens Iron*, is taken from Proverbs 27:17. I hope to show how common men, filled with love for their Savior, Jesus Christ, have sharpened my life. I introduce each of them--but only briefly. Their personal testimony will give substance to the life-sharpening qualities Christ used to draw me closer to Him.

I write this book with the prayer of the Psalmist on my lips: "Not to us, O Lord, not to us, but to your name be the glory because of your loving kindness and truth" (Psalm 115.1 NAS).

1

Warren Hardig

*T*he testimony of an eyewitness has powerful impact in a court of law. It can sway the jury's decision and thus determine the outcome of an entire case. In fact, a witness can make the difference between life or death for the accused through his statements. Our legal system is built around the power of a firsthand report.

In much the same way God's system for reclaiming His lost world depends to a large extent on the power of a witness. He has ordained that witnesses should be in the front lines of the battle for minds and hearts of this world's people. Jesus commissioned His disciples (and us) to be "witnesses unto me in Jerusalem (your home town), Judea (nearby areas with the same culture), and Samaria (a different culture), and unto the uttermost parts of the world."

Apart from Jesus Christ, I have no reason nor authority to compile this book. Actually, neither I nor the other men you'll meet in the pages ahead would have a story worthy of print except for our personal encounter with Him.

Space and vocabulary prohibit telling all God has done for me personally. My own limited vision of the spiritual world keeps me from even seeing it all. However, when I get to heaven and discover the full extent of God's mercy in my behalf, I shall join the multitudes in singing praises to the King of Kings and Lord of Lords.

My prayer is that the Holy Spirit will anoint each testimony in such a way that lives around the world will be changed--giving full proof that "iron sharpens iron, so one man sharpens another" (Proverbs 27:17). Let me begin with what happened to me:

Good Ole Boys
Don't Go To Heaven

by Warren Hardig

My wife, Velma, has always been a step or two ahead of me. I spend a good part of my life trying to keep up. So that Saturday evening in 1969 when she decided we ought to attend a Men For Missions banquet, I was far from excited. Frankly, I had my fill of those fund-raising dinners. Even more important, this was the night for "Gunsmoke." I wanted to spend my evening watching Matt Dillon and Miss Kitty, not in some stuffy meeting room sandwiched between people I didn't know and would never see again.

But when Velma sets her mind to something she's not easily denied, so in the end I reluctantly consented. The menu was the usual rubbery fried chicken, and the speaker was a former insurance executive named Harry Burr. I looked at my watch. "Surely," I thought, "I'll be out of here in a couple of hours."

But this meeting was different. Harry oozed excitement and that surprised me. Most of the banquets I had attended were dull, dull, dull. He began by telling of a man named Clark Erdley. Long past his retirement, Clark heard that OMS International needed a maintenance man at its world headquarters in Greenwood, Indiana. He'd not ventured much farther than the smoke from his chimney--never outside his home state of Pennsylvania. But this shy, reticent man left his beloved farm to give his remaining years in missionary service. Not wanting pay or recognition, he went for the express purpose of giving homage to Christ. Although he had little education and few skills, he knew how to mop floors, wash windows, and clean toilets. So he kept the mission headquarters shining. He also quietly depleted his life-savings, giving generously to advance the Gospel across the world. Never wavering, never complaining, he just worked and gave his all for Christ, year after year. Affectionately known as "Uncle Clark," he worked at the Mission until age and infirmities made it impossible. "How could any of us live a more fruitful life," asked Harry, "than to give all we have--our money, our possessions, our skills and abilities, our time, our very lives to Jesus Christ--just like Uncle Clark Erdley?"

My heart was pounding--I didn't like what I was hearing. It made me feel guilty. I was seeking the golden ring, not servanthood. If you would have asked me to characterize my life in a single word, I would have used the word *more*--more money, more investments, more security, more pleasure. After all, I planned to retire at age 50 so I could devote the rest of my life to hunting and fishing. "Is this what religion is all about?" I wondered.

I was relieved when Harry dropped that subject and turned to something I could handle. He began telling how

Men For Missions took large numbers of laymen on crusades to Brazil, Haiti, Colombia, and other OMS mission fields. Then he asked for everyone who had been on an MFM crusade to stand. I couldn't believe what I saw-- almost half of the people there were on their feet. A few even gave testimonies, telling how those crusades had completely changed their lives.

Now I was getting interested. I suppose Velma knew I would. This *was* something different and it *did* appeal to me. I could see myself heading into the jungles of South America to help missionaries and build churches. It had all the ingredients of an adventure novel. It fit my macho image and would allow me to serve the Lord. I was particularly interested in doing something significant because I had only recently been converted from a dreadful past of smoking, drinking, and gambling. Now I was learning how to live for Jesus. Right then and there I decided to go on a crusade, little dreaming what it would set in motion. But first I want to tell you how I happened to be in that meeting.

I was born on a farm near Newton, Illinois. My parents were honest, hard-working people who seldom, if ever, went to church. But that doesn't mean they didn't try to live decent lives. In fact, they worked very hard to ensure that my brother and I had strong moral standards. From a very early age I was taught not to lie, cheat, or steal, that my word is my bond, and that women should be treated with respect (any kind of sexual immorality would have brought about devastating punishment).   I never resisted these mandates--it's just that I didn't know there were spiritual requirements as well. Later in life I often referred to my early level of spiritual knowledge by saying, "Velma and the pastor had to work with me for a year to bring me up to zero."

As an ambitious young farm boy I wanted to join the Future Farmers of America. To my dismay, however, the application form asked a prickly question: "What church do you attend?" Eager to qualify, I decided to become a church-goer, a diversion I found increasingly enjoyable when I met a cute little freshman there named Velma Williams. Our first date was on a hayride sponsored by the church's youth group.

Velma came from solid Scottish stock and a fine Christian home. She accepted Jesus as her Savior at age 12. It happened one Sunday after she heard a sermon on Jesus teaching Nicodemus the meaning and significance of being born again. While she was bouncing a ball against the house that afternoon, the concept suddenly became clear to her. She stopped playing, went inside, and while her parents were in the barn milking she knelt by the sofa and gave her heart to Christ.

At this point in my life I didn't even know the Bible had different chapters, but I saw nothing but good in this new and fragile relationship with Velma Williams. By joining the church, I not only could enhance my standing in the FFA but also impress Velma at the same time.

After graduation from high school, I joined the army reserves and was assigned to a six-month stint with the Engineer Corps at Ft. Belvoire, Virginia. Here my bad habits took on new proportions. Along with my regular intake of liquor, I began smoking several packs of cigarettes a day and developed a rich, new vocabulary. I also attained great proficiency at poker--so much so that I became the envy of my buddies. You name it--five card draw, stud, straight, or wild--I mastered them all and gained the label of "card shark." In the midst of all this, however, I was curiously haunted by a fear of death that never seemed to desert me.

Two years after my discharge in 1959, Velma and I were married. She worked as a cosmetologist and later became the administrative secretary to a number of doctors in a medical clinic. I found a position with Coca-Cola, then switched to a management position in a fertilizer company owned by Standard Oil.

Things were going well, or so it seemed. We began to accumulate our share of material possessions. I took a particular fancy to guns, acquiring an impressive collection. Meanwhile we were careful to keep up appearances at church. Despite my cavernous ignorance of the Bible, I "taught" a Sunday school class and served on the board. Always generous by nature, I gave groceries and money to needy families in the community. This not only soothed my conscience, but allowed me the luxury of believing generosity to be certain evidence of my Christianity. It also helped satisfy my self-image--I wanted to be known and admired as a "good ole boy".

At the same time, however, I maintained an entirely different set of friends. They knew me as a social-drinking, foul-mouthed, four-pack-a-day smoker who had an explosive temper. I not only gave the impression that life was one big party, I made that my goal. I rejected sexual immorality, however, primarily because of my upbringing. Religion? Well, it was okay for women and kids, but keep it away from me. "A place for everything, and everything in its place," I thought, and all my pieces fit together just fine.

Living a double life is not easy, however. Ever tried it? The longer it goes on the more complicated it gets, and as it becomes more intricate it takes more effort to keep it afloat. All this began closing in on me. For example, I worried about going to church on Sunday morning with Saturday night's breath. Then there were the never-ending poker games--once inside the tavern I was safe, but I never knew who saw me enter or leave. At first I just had headaches, but then I began suffering from exhaustion, and diarrhea plagued me. If that weren't enough, my cigarette habit produced a chronic cough and lung problems. Then, to add insult to injury, I began to look prematurely old and haggard.

A disturbing (but life-saving) change in this pattern emerged in the autumn of 1967 when Velma rededicated herself to the Lord during a revival. Soon after, I sensed an uncomfortable breach in our marriage. I would watch her read the Bible for hours--with an earnestness I had never seen before. My first reaction was to humor her. So I bought her a beautiful Thompson Chain Reference Bible. When I saw her on her knees one day, however, I knew we were worlds apart. To make matters worse, I strongly suspected she was praying for me, her wayward husband.

Then in the spring of the year my father died--while digging the grave of a friend. Mother cried and friends cried. But I didn't have a tear in me. It was not because I didn't love my dad, I just didn't experience the emotions that make one cry. My rationale was swift and simple: Men don't cry. I'm a man, therefore I don't cry.

The preacher did a good job with the funeral service, and I developed a closeness with him during those days. That, along with Velma's rededication, made me more susceptible to religion than ever before.

Our pastor was a real born-again Christian. He often spoke to me about my smoking habit, but I was always ready with an answer. "It's no problem for me," I argued.

"But will you at least pray about it?" he challenged.

"Okay," I agreed, "I'll pray about it if you will."

"I have been," he retorted; "I wonder when you'll start."

That night I surprised myself by remembering my promise. I got down on my knees to straighten this issue out once and for all. "Lord," I began, "these people are hassling me about my smoking. You know it's no big deal, but if You don't mind, would You please get them off my back and show them I'm right?"

One morning a few weeks later, with a cigarette between my lips and a cup of steaming coffee at my side, I casually picked up the new Bible I'd given Velma. Thumbing through it to what appeared to be an interesting part, I began reading.

Suddenly, almost audibly, a voice thundered in my ear, *"Why are you still smoking when your wife and pastor are praying for you?"* I was terrified.

The pressure was on! God was dealing with me and I knew it. I was frightened--perhaps frantic is a better word. I jumped in my pick-up and drove to the local filling station, my usual supplier of cigarettes. Walking up to the counter, I plunked down two quarters and with determination in my eyes bought a pack of Kent filter-tips, my favorite brand. Then I turned to the attendant and with dramatic flair held the cigarettes at his eye level. "See this pack of cigarettes?" I said. "This is the last one I'll ever buy."

He smiled, and went about his business. God's grace *was* at work in my life, however. It was powerful, and I could feel Him drawing me closer. Still, I knew that an act of self-reform, even giving up my beloved cigarettes, was not enough to put me on good terms with God.

The Holy Spirit continued His tug as I drove to my office at the fertilizer plant. Upon arrival I went directly to my office, shut the door, and got on my knees behind my desk. "Lord," I cried, "I don't have to tell You that I am a sinner. You know that as well as I do. Forgive me of my sins and take cigarettes out of my life. We both know I can't quit on my own." Then I added, "God, would you come into my life and live through me, so I really can be a Christian? I am utterly powerless to live this Christian life by myself."

Suddenly I felt entirely new and clean, just as though I'd taken a spiritual bath. I was newly clothed in the righteousness of Jesus Christ and all desire for cigarettes was gone-- totally gone. With a "good riddance" on my lips, I threw the pack of Kents into a clover field. I never smoked again from that day to this.

Driving home that day, I basked in the wonderful, divine peace that permeated my whole being. Then I got on the phone to tell our pastor what God had done. For some reason he was skeptical. But the change was real, beyond dispute, and Velma soon noticed it. My health improved dramatically as the stomach troubles, diarrhea, and stress symptoms began to disappear.

Velma and I started working together as a team. Among other things we took an active part in the youth program of our church. At our first camp five of the kids accepted Christ as their Savior. How we loved those young people. Almost every week we saw at least one or more of them turn their lives over to the Lord.

Though very zealous, I was a babe in Christ. The Lord still needed to deal with several areas of my life. It's so easy to give Jesus just part of yourself, thinking He will be satisfied and allow you to hold on to the rest. I was soon to learn that He wants *all* of you--every fiber of your being, every thought in your mind, your will, your heart, and your soul.

Then one day some of Velma's relatives (oil field workers from Wyoming) came to visit. Before long I heard one of them say, "Let's go have a beer." I didn't have the nerve to stand my ground and say no, so within an hour I was sitting at the bar.

Suddenly the Lord reminded me that a girl in our youth group, who I was trying to win to Christ, came from an alcoholic family. "What would she think," the Holy Spirit whispered, "if she were to see you coming out of this tavern? What kind of testimony would you have with her?"

Sitting on that bar stool, I realized that *my* drinking could cause someone *else* to stumble. I recalled how this young girl would cling to Velma and me--resisting all efforts to send her back into that alcoholic homelife. Right then and there I resolved to never touch another drop of liquor. Shoving my glass away, I paid my bill, and talked Velma's relatives into leaving. It was a resolution that by God's grace I have kept.

Some time later I got involved in a heated political discussion. Has that ever happened to you? Becoming more and more agitated, I suddenly lost control and let out a profane oath. No sooner had it left my lips than I felt a deep sense of shame and regret, a feeling I never want to experience again. I had betrayed my Lord and put my Christian testimony in jeopardy.

I had heard of the doctrine of sanctification, a deeper work of grace whereby God's Spirit deals with the old sin nature. Until that time it had been nothing more than a nice teaching, but in that instant I realized how desperately I needed it.

Fearful of a broken relationship with God I went home, got on my knees, and prayed, "I don't know what causes me to lose control of my temper, Lord, but if You'll take that problem from me, I'll serve You *faithfully*." Mentally I inventoried all the important things in my life--my house, car, bank account, guns--even Velma. To that list I also added my membership in the Masonic Lodge (I'd been in the order for years, attained the 32nd degree, and proudly wore my lodge ring). "Lord, I'll give You all these things--everything I possess. Help me to put You first in my life. I never want to feel that I've betrayed You again."

True to His Word, God's Spirit filled me. He not only took away my vile temper and evil habits, but also gave me a whole new set of priorities--like Bible study, routine prayer, and devotions. That's how I happened to be at a Men For Missions banquet to hear a man named Harry Burr--and ended up promising the Lord I'd go to Haiti on a crusade.

Before I joined the team of MFMers bound for Haiti, I specifically asked the Lord to let me lead one Haitian to Him. I received that privilege, plus a whole lot more. God turned my value system upside down. No longer did the word "more" characterize my life. Before Haiti, things (possessions) owned me; after Haiti, God owned me and everything I'd acquired.

One hot, breezeless afternoon, our crusade trudged up a mountain trail toward a place called Grand Ravine. Sweating profusely, OMS missionary Flo Boyer and I were bringing up the rear. Along the way I surveyed this incredibly poor section of Haiti. We passed Haitian "homes" which were nothing but crude huts without walls. Naked children played around charcoal cooking fires, and old men sat in the shade, playing cards and passing time until they died.

While I followed the rugged path with Flo, two Haitians approached us. One of them, his decrepit frame draped in filthy rags, was the most hopeless creature I'd ever seen. His companion addressed Flo. "This man heard about your group," he said, "and wants to become a Christian."

I looked around, then down--the man was on his knees. Peering up at us through bushy eyebrows, he displayed a forlorn expression I'll never forget.

With Flo as my interpreter, I proceeded to explain the New Birth to this poor man. When I finished, Flo and I prayed, then the kneeling man--in a simple petition--invited Jesus into his heart. Rising to his feet he gave me a beautiful smile. Flo said she thought the conversion was genuine because his countenance completely changed. How faithful God had been--to both of us.

After we boarded the bus for our return trip I glanced over my shoulder, and there he was! The man I had led to the Lord was just behind me and on the opposite side of the aisle. Now I noticed he was clean, dressed in respectable clothing, and wearing a radiant expression.

I didn't know what to say and I knew he couldn't understand English anyway. So I just pointed to my chest and said, "You have the love of Christ in your heart, don't you?"

Without breaking his broad smile, he pulled out a Bible and joyfully shook it a few times. God had cut across racial, language, cultural, and economic lines to speak to this poor peasant in Haiti just as He spoke to me, a farm boy from southern Illinois. I was beginning to realize what it was all about, and that it was *real*.

That trip to Haiti literally changed my life. I had always prided myself on being a tough, macho type, but Haiti broke by heart. Haiti is where I learned to cry. It taught me the meaning of a lost world.

Later I learned that the man's name was Massillion. After returning to Illinois I received a letter from Flo. I read it while sitting on my tractor. She said, "Warren, Massillion wants to give me his daughter. He knows I would take good care of her and provide her with an education." This act of faith really tugged at my heart.

Velma and I discussed it in depth and prayed about it for days. We realized Massillion must love his daughter very much to consider giving her to Flo for a better life. We finally concluded that we could influence this situation by paying for part of her education. This allowed her to remain with her family and still go to school.

My next contact with Massillion did not come until 1974. But at the time, with awe and wonder, I realized that God answered my prayer and gave me a bonus: one Haitian, for one star in my crown.

Missions was now a priority for Velma and me. I joined the MFM council in our southern Illinois area. Then in 1973 National Director Howard Young asked me to join OMS as the MFM regional director. This was a terrifying prospect. Years earlier I had thought of missionaries as incompetent misfits--people who went to foreign countries because they couldn't make it at home. Now that I had met so many of them, I could hardly imagine myself worthy to join their ranks.

For two nights I was unable to sleep. As I tossed and turned, words from I Samuel 15:22 kept coming to mind:

"Obedience is better than sacrifice." A short time later at an OMS conference, Helmut Schultz, a missionary to Japan, rose to speak. "For my text," he began, "I want you to turn to I Samuel 15:22." His words melted the remnants of my human resistance. God used Helmut and Massillion, the Haitian beggar, to cause me to be a missionary. We joined OMS.

In 1974, during my first year as regional director, the Lord sent another bonus--the opportunity to lead a crusade to Haiti. I wondered if I'd be able to find Massillion among the millions who inhabit the island. Had he moved away? Was he still alive?

When we reached Cap-Haitien the missionaries suggested that I announce my presence over the OMS Christian radio station, 4VEH. They were sure Massillion, or some of his family, would hear the Creole broadcast. He did.

Massillion came with his wife and 16-year-old son. They walked ten miles under a scorching Haitian sun to get to 4VEH and the OMS compound. We immediately recognized each other. Different languages prevented verbal communication, but Massillion found a way. I was elated when he pointed to me, folded his hands as if in prayer, then pointed to the mountains where he had been saved. Big smiles and hearty handshakes were the order of the hour.

Massillion and family went to church with us that night, and through our interpreter he told me his wife wanted a

Bible. I didn't have an extra Bible with me so I told him I'd give her one the next day.

That night I climbed into a soft bed and covered myself with a percale sheet. I felt satisfied; after all, had I not sacrificed myself and accomplished great things?

Unknown to me, Massillion and his family slept on the ground outside the compound. After brushing away the rocks they covered themselves with banana leaves--waiting for tomorrow when his wife would get the desire of her heart, a Bible.

The next morning I ate my pride for breakfast.

In addition to the Bible I gave them money for food and clothing. But on that day I received another surprise; Massillion and his "wife" were not married. Although not right, it *was* explainable. The average annual income for a Haitian was $95 and legal fees associated with a wedding cost $45--half a year's salary. I also discovered that Massillion had 12 children. I knew I wouldn't feel right if I allowed them to live together like this, so I gave them enough for the wedding, and an extra amount for two wedding rings, a wedding dress, and two pairs of shoes.

There is no doubt that Massillion had a profound effect on my life. When I returned to southern Illinois, I came across Acts 15:9:

"He made no distinction between us and them, for he purified their hearts by faith."

I then envisioned a farm boy from southern Illinois and a dirt farmer from Haiti with 12 kids, strolling along golden streets of heaven, side by side. I didn't need a Harvard scholar to sharpen my life--all it took was a poverty-stricken beggar.

Since then I've enjoyed a wonderful and productive life with Men For Missions. I served as MFM regional director from 1973 to 1982. We then moved to the OMS/MFM headquarters at Greenwood, Indiana where I assumed the position of national director. In 1983 I was elected to the position of international executive director--stepping into the shoes of Harry Burr, that fellow who spoke at my initiation to MFM.

When I trace my life back to the moment I knelt behind my desk in that fertilizer plant, I am absolutely amazed at God's grace. He has taken this country boy all over the globe in His service. I've visited scores of countries and fellowshiped with His choicest people. I've had the privilege of witnessing to thousands and seeing many of them come to Christ. One particular highlight was the Penetration '79 Crusade to Ecuador, where it was my joy to lead 33 Ecuadorians to Christ. But an equal thrill has come from involving hundreds of laymen in firsthand experiences on OMS mission fields. That's an impact that not only transformed their lives but those of their families and the countless number to whom they've witnessed in other lands.

Yes, I wanted to watch "Gunsmoke" that evening in 1969. I wanted to see Matt Dillon and his side-kick, Chester, round up the bad guys. But the Lord, acting through my faithful wife, Velma, had different plans for me. How grateful I am. A single television show traded for all that's happened since that night! Believe me, you'll never win a pot like that in a poker game.

2

Harry Burr

*O*n a recent trip to India, I witnessed many of her 760 million wearing the mark of Hinduism on their bodies. A red dot on the forehead, multi-colored stripes decorating the face, bands of color displayed elsewhere--all proclaiming belief and loyalty. But in the midst of this screaming array of identity marks, I also saw deep despair. The bright hues of their painted bodies only served to mask their hopelessness. Comfort in their man-made, lifeless idols, could not be found.

Even more heartrending was the realization that they did not know their dedication was useless, their gods unhearing. As Paul proclaimed to the men of Athens (Acts 17:23), so I wanted to say to India's people:

"Men of India, I see in every way that you are religious, for as I walked around and looked carefully at your objects of worship, I even found an altar with the inscription: To An Unknown God."

In spite of the despair, however, I couldn't ignore their boldness. Returning to my home church I took my seat in a cushioned pew. As I looked around, anger welled deep within me. "Where is the courage of my fellow Christians?" I asked myself.

I was appeased only by recalling the few who have given sacrificially--those who have not bowed to the false gods of American materialism but serve Christ with impassioned resolve.

One such man is Harry Burr. My priorities changed the first time I heard him speak (see Chapter One). His effect on me was continuous, too. It almost came to the point that I feared listening to him--for each time I did, God altered my life.

A native of Michigan, Harry led Men For Missions for 23 years. It's impossible to capture the epic history of the incidents and adventures in this man's life. Chronicled here is what I persuaded him to tell of his service to God and the events which led to the rich heritage of Men For Missions.

Called to Belong to Jesus

by Harry Burr

World War II brought many changes in my life. But I must admit it was kind to me. Although often placed in harm's way, I was never injured nor traumatized.

Fresh out of high school in 1942, I joined the Navy and was assigned to the Merchant Marines. The war was at its peak and manpower at a premium. Men were released from prison to serve in the armed forces. It was a tough crowd but I was a tough marine. I even participated in shipboard boxing contests.

We carried ammunition from the United States to northern Africa by way of the Mediterranean Sea. On the return trip we transported German prisoners. I remember one run quite well. We were in battle with German aircraft. Bombs were bursting all around, and with each close hit a terrible concussion sent the whole ship into colossal reverberation. We expected to take a direct hit any moment.

Then came my time for duty in the hold, deep within our battered ship. Heading down the ladder I gave my life preserver to the sailor I was relieving. This was standard procedure; in the engine room life preservers were totally worthless.

A few steps further I met one of the convicts who chose the service over prison. A big bruiser, he was a gambler, wrestler, and ruffian, all rolled into one. Suddenly he blocked my way. As the ship recoiled from the bursting bombs, he said, "I noticed something, Burr. You've got a Bible in your sea bag. You must know something about religion; why don't you tell us what to do, like right now?"

I had a Bible all right--only because my mother insisted. Squeezing past him I said, "Hey man, I'm not even a Christian. How can I tell you what to do?"

I knew each rung of that ladder lessened my chances of survival. The air was sour and stale, and the noise of the exploding bombs terrorized me. In my panic I thought a prayer might be in order. "Lord," I begged, "if You'll just get me on dry land I'll give You my life."

We escaped destruction and a loving Father lived up to His part of my request. When we pulled into an Algerian port, however, I forgot my promise and had a high ole time.

In July 1944 our ship, the *S.S. Jonathan Trumbull*, was back in the U.S. to be loaded with supplies for Murmansk, Russia. The ship's inspectors caused a long delay in our departure date, so I decided to take my 30-day leave. I headed for Detroit to visit my parents.

When I arrived my mother handed me an old, unopened letter from the Navy. It was orders transferring me from the European to the Pacific theater of war. Only by taking my leave did I learn of this transfer. Now I couldn't return to the *S.S. Trumbull*, without being AWOL from my "official" duty. My buddies would have to sail without me.

To clear up the problem I reported to my new assignment almost immediately. About 50 days later a letter and newspaper clipping from my mother shook me to the depths of my being. The *S.S. Jonathan Trumbull* had been sunk off the shores of Russia in the Barents Sea. The entire crew went down.

The ship I loved had become a steel coffin. Death had brushed me aside while sweeping the others into a frigid grave. But in my spiritually dead state, I only marveled at my "luck", not realizing that God was at work in my life.

My new assignment was to a naval LST scheduled for an invasion of Korea. But the war ended, and our job changed to repatriation of Japanese, Koreans, and Chinese to their respective countries.

In each port I spent time exploring the countries. I'll never forget the scenes in China. I watched as bodies of starvation victims were loaded on ancient, bloodstained wagons. Creaking down rough streets, they dripped body fluids all the way to huge common graves. People came for miles to look for their loved ones. But any corpse not claimed by day's end--well, in it went.

If nothing else, I gained compassion during those trips. One day when the cooks dumped our huge quantities of garbage over the side, I looked below. There, like flies buzzing rotten meat, boat people descended on the scraps.

Scooping them from the water with nets, they ate them on the spot.

I cried. Something had to be done, but what? After days of thought and numerous deadends, I devised a plan. With the help of my buddies, food remaining on trays was sorted into boxes--bread in one, meat in another, and so on. Then assembling individual box lunches we provided "unsoaked" meals for the Chinese. After that some guys started saving half their ration in order to share more with those starving masses.

Pleased with our success, we devised a better deal. Why not have the Chinese clean bilges, mop decks, and do all our undesirable chores? Instead of paying them, however, we let them eat our lunch. Everyone benefited from that arrangement.

I had started out hating Orientals. Weren't they part of the reason I had to be away from home? But now I was feeding them! I think God was shaping me for when He'd let me share with them the Bread of Life.

Finally, my service tenure ended. Homecoming was wonderful. With my whole life ahead of me, I had places to go and people to see. Wanting to take advantage of the GI bill, I started checking out colleges with good football teams. My mother, however, had other ideas. She quietly prayed that I'd attend a Christian school.

To my surprise, every place I tried was already full. Finally, at mother's suggestion, I found an opening at Spring

Arbor College in Michigan. You guessed it--a liberal arts school with a Christian emphasis.

Arriving at Spring Arbor, I discovered that no smoking or drinking were allowed on campus. That certainly wasn't for me. So, immediately renting a house in town, I proceeded to load the refrigerator with beer.

Upon finding other students of my style, I rented the extra bedrooms to them. Before long the place earned its reputation as "the party house." Then the college president invited me to his office.

He was soft spoken and gentle, but made his message clear. "You can live off campus and what you do there is up to you, but the minute you step on campus you'd better be straight. If I see you with liquor or cigarettes, you're finished at Spring Arbor."

After four years in the Navy I understood that kind of language. I knew he was a man I could respect. "If that's what you require," I said, "that's exactly what you'll get." We got along fine after that.

I ate most of my meals at the school and began noticing a group of students praying during lunch. I discovered they were targeting the non-Christians on campus. One day I passed an open window and heard them praying for *me*. That was a shocker! I thought about it for weeks. By the end of the semester I moved onto campus.

My life was like a marble rolling downhill. In spite of my momentum, things kept getting in the way--redirecting my course. I blamed the Orientals for my war years but wound up feeding them; I wanted to enter a "football" college, but ended up at a Christian school; I wanted to live in a party house, but was now on campus abstaining from liquor and cigarettes. Once channeled, however, I seemed to accept my new direction without resistance. I think God was getting me ready to meet Eleanor.

She sat in front of me in chemistry lab. While the professor explained atoms and nuclei, I admired her beautiful hair. When the lecture got into acids and the elements, I was working on my opening line. But, I knew my chances were slim to none. She was one of the top girls in school. She always got A's, and everything she did was perfect.

Then came Christmas vacation. We all headed home and I was really looking forward to New Year's Eve.

Before the war, at our final New Year's Eve party a group of us guys from high school decided we'd throw another party, a big one, when we got back. I think it was our way of ensuring our lives against what was ahead. The party was scheduled for this New Year's Eve--1946.

Most of the old gang was there. A few had been killed, several had traded arms and legs for the freedom they gallantly defended. One was blind. Others had shrapnel wounds--some seemed distant and withdrawn. Surveying this pathetic group, I recalled my months of combat and the death and destruction that surrounded me. Suddenly in the midst of the party's noise and confusion, God's voice came through loud and clear: "I spared you for a purpose."

It was almost midnight, but I was oblivious to the party. I was to ring in the New Year by leading the group in a toast, but now.... The clock began striking. Eight, nine--the crowd roared--ten, eleven--glasses were held high. As the clock struck the magic hour I scanned the group of merry-makers. Instead of launching them on a drinking binge, I spoiled their party.

"You know," I said, "my parents took most of you to Sunday school at some point in your life, and you heard about Jesus Christ. I decided tonight not to live like this anymore. I'm going to become a Christian, and I invite you to join me as I leave."

No one did.

A captive of the Holy Spirit, I made my way home, went directly to my bedroom and knelt to firmly commit my life to Christ. When I looked out the window it seemed that pine boughs blowing in the wind were clapping for joy.

I didn't tell my mother, but I think she knew. On fledgling legs, I wanted to be sure I could live this Christian life before I told anyone.

Back at Spring Arbor, a friend caught me reading the Bible. "What are you doing, man?" he blurted.

Forced from my secret service, I said boldly, even surprising myself, "Look, Larry, I accepted Christ while home on vacation."

"I thought you were acting strange," he said. "Your language is different and you've not smoked, even off campus. I've been wondering about you."

"Larry, I feel the Lord wants me to make a public confession at church next Sunday. But I need some support. Will you go with me?"

"Yeah. I'll go to the church--just don't ask me to go forward."

Sunday finally came. Larry, true to his word, showed up in his only suit, a two-tone brown herringbone with wide lapels. I straightened his tie. We piled into the car and headed for church.

I knew the altar call followed the sermon, and on this Sunday the preacher didn't know when to stop. After what seemed hours, he did a five-minute windup and made his appeal. My heart was pounding, my palms were wet, and my mouth dry enough to spit cotton. But I began the long walk down the center aisle, unaware of anything or anyone--just my target, the altar. Falling on my knees, I prayed, "O Lord, forgive my sins. Please come live your life through me."

Preoccupied with prayer and my salvation, I didn't notice what was happening around me. I soon learned that 40 students followed me to the altar. Even Larry, the last holdout, joined them in commitment to Christ. It was like a revival. I was so thrilled I couldn't contain myself. After my past life, how could God use me in such a miraculous way?

A month or two later a terrible snow storm left a Greyhound bus stranded in front of the college. We gave up our beds in the dorms for the passengers. Since we were in a revival, we invited them to come. The Holy Spirit came, too, and over half of that group--even the bus driver--accepted Christ. It was a great time.

That summer I worked in Detroit, commuting from my parents' home in Ferndale. Just as I got off the bus at the Greyhound station one morning, who should be stepping from another but Eleanor! She was enroute to a summer job in Indiana and had 20 minutes before her next bus. I'll never know how, but I mustered enough courage to ask her for a date--for the all-school picnic when school resumed in the fall. She accepted! I glided back to my office nine inches off the ground. "I'm going to marry that girl," I declared!

After a wonderful courtship, we married in 1949 and spent our first years in Temperance, Michigan, just north of Toledo. While Eleanor taught school, I trained for and entered the insurance business. Both of us took active roles in Youth for Christ (YFC) and the church, where my brother, Larry, pastored.

In 1951 our YFC sponsored an area revival. Dr. Dwight Ferguson, whom we'd never seen nor heard--was to be the evangelist. In a big tent we'd hoisted in the local park, his fiery exhortations brought scores running to the altar every night.

Dwight stayed in our home those ten days and became a regular visitor whenever traveling through and needing a bed. Soon after the revival he went to India and saw multitudes living in spiritual darkness. His heart was broken. That's when he put missions on the front burner and later founded Men For Missions.

After that, whenever he dropped by our home, he'd leave the Bible on the coffee table open to Psalms 2:8, "Ask of Me and I will give you the heathen for your inheritance." Beside it was his note: "Why don't you?"

Also during that revival in Temperance, Michigan, CBMC (Christian Business Men's Committee) took an active role. They really had a burden for souls--even rounded up drunks on the street and took them to prayer meetings.

One morning I went to their CBMC breakfast. The speaker, Waldo Yeager, quoted Romans 12:1, "Therefore, I urge you, brothers, in view of God's mercy, to offer your bodies as living sacrifices, holy and pleasing to God--this is your spiritual act of worship" (NIV). Waldo then asked a pointed question: "What does that verse mean to you?"

As I thought about it, deep conviction engulfed me. My commitment included only comfortable, self-gratifying involvement. My life, my job, my home, my wife, my future, all I had was *mine*. But that morning I recognized what God desires and requires. With all my heart I turned everything, even my new car, over to *Him*. Unfortunately, the car rolled back off the altar the next night at a church board meeting.

Asked to pick up some children down muddy country roads each Sunday, I rebelled inside. Why couldn't some farmer with a beat-up jalopy get those kids?

Too embarrassed to refuse, however, I trekked those rutted miles to crowd 13 rowdy ragamuffins into my two-door sedan. Talk about a mess! When I got home that automobile looked like a mobile slum. "That's it! Never again!" I ranted. In between my ravings, Eleanor wedged a few choice words: "I thought that was the Lord's car," she chirped. Needless to say, the next Sunday I made my rounds again--and many times thereafter. Within a few months we had to buy a bus to bring in all the children.

Fifteen years later I was the missionary speaker for a Kansas church conference. On Sunday morning the sharp young pastor introduced me. "Folks," he said, "our speaker today is the man who drove many times down a muddy country road in Michigan to get me into Sunday school." At that moment the dirty fingerprints, chewed bubble gum, mud and candy smears in my car became very worthwhile.

How I happened to be a missionary speaker, though, goes back to Dwight Ferguson. He urged us to attend a missionary conference of OMS International, the organization he had joined. It was held in Winona Lake, Indiana. We went that June and were deeply moved. Missionary speakers pleaded for workers to help with their overwhelming task. When we heard that over 90% of the world had less than 5% of the Christian witness, we were ready to sign up.

Of course we had no Bible training, so offered to support ourselves overseas and assist the missionaries with menial tasks and business affairs. But that was before Men For Missions was founded, opening the door for lay people to serve on the fields.

Discouraged from pursuing that objective, we left the conference disappointed. Perhaps the Lord wanted us to stay in business and help missionaries by giving money. So that's exactly what we did for the next five years. Our business grew along with our commitment to Christ. Appointed as youth leaders in our denomination, we traveled to different cities on weekends and organized 36 youth groups in local churches. This led to starting a youth camp near Jackson, Michigan. It was a tremendous success and affected the lives of hundreds of young people. We didn't want to leave.

But leave we did. My company transferred me to Findlay, Ohio, as a district manager. We built a three-bedroom home with a breezeway leading to a two-car garage. We even bought a new car to match the house--one of those '57 Plymouths with big tailfins and push-button transmission. To help me in the office, Eleanor didn't resume teaching. We joined an aggressive church and life was good.

One of my jobs was training salesmen. At a company convention in Marshall, Michigan, I was to challenge my colleagues on the ways to produce successful agencies.

"Salesmen must spend less time with their families,"

I stressed. "Take less time for recreation, work harder, and sell more insurance. Then we'll all make more money."

During a sleepless night the Lord reminded me that my speech certainly didn't track with Romans 12:1, my life verse. I was urging men toward the wrong goals.

During devotions the next morning I felt deeply the Spirit's leading to quit the insurance business and give my time to Christian service. Eleanor backed me all the way as I called my boss and told him of my decision. He listened in disbelief. "You just need some time off, Harry. You've been working too hard. We're prepared to give you a higher salary, as well."

I didn't accept his offer, yet had no idea what I was to do. Of course I felt an obligation to the three agents whose livelihood depended on me. But God provides when He leads. All of them found immediate employment elsewhere.

The next night Eleanor and I drove to a Men For Missions banquet in Dayton, Ohio. As we walked into the hotel, Enloe Wallar, a charter MFMer, met us at the door. "Harry, it's great to see you. Could I ask you a question?"

"Sure, Enloe--why not?"

"Have you ever considered quitting your job with the insurance company and coming with OMS?"

Of course Enloe didn't know I had just resigned. He teased me about my response for years, and I guess I was toying with him a bit when I said, "Well, I'll pray about it."

The next afternoon I was asked to accompany 15 men to the clothing store of Nate Scharff, there in Dayton, for prayer. We went to a second-floor room and although we prayed for almost two hours, it seemed like 20 minutes. We were the recipients of a wonderful outpouring of the Holy Spirit, and during that time God sealed a decision in my heart. We would join OMS.

Of course, the OMS Board had to approve our application. Nevertheless, we were so certain we were in God's will we put our house up for sale, went to the OMS office in Winona Lake, Indiana and offered ourselves for work. For the next few weeks we drove back and forth to Findlay on weekends to oversee our property and continue church duties. On April 7, 1957, our application was approved.

Eleanor walked away from the beautiful home she had always wanted and followed me to a single room in a home occupied by a family of six. Shortly thereafter, she became seriously ill. Doctors treated her with 13 shots of penicillin before discovering she was allergic to it. The penicillin resulted in terrible swelling--so much so they feared for her life.

At the same time a missionary borrowed my new Plymouth. Calling from Columbus, Ohio, she told me everyone was okay, but the car was wrecked. Two days later another missionary, driving Eleanor's car, threw a rod through the block ruining the engine. It seemed that everything was going wrong. A number of our Christian friends felt that the Lord was trying to tell us we'd made a mistake.

In her hospital room, I asked Eleanor how she felt about it. Tears rolled from the sides of her tightly swollen eyes as she said, "I've never felt more at peace. I believe we're in the center of God's will."

That was all I needed. Back at my desk, I knelt and recommitted everything to the Lord. Then came a switch in strategy. Instead of attacking us, Satan tried to tempt us.

Our church in Findlay asked us to return, offering me an associate pastor's position. In fact, they would even pay off the mortgage on our new home. I must admit, it was very enticing. But after prayer, we saw the issue from God's perspective. Wasn't the church praying, "God, send the Burrs back to us," rather than, "God, help them do Your will"?

From then on, the matter was settled in our hearts. Eleanor was released from the hospital, an OMS apartment became available, and insurance covered our car repairs. The only problem left was the upkeep and payments on our unsold house.

We returned to Findlay to attend the church picnic on Independence Day. Enroute we stopped at the real estate office. The realtor was all smiles. "Well, folks, your house sold yesterday--a cash deal--for more than your asking price."

Needless to say, we were elated as we arrived at the picnic. Upon announcing our good news, however, a disapproving silence fell over the crowd. For them, the unsold house was the Lord's clear sign that we should forget OMS and return to Findlay.

On Sunday the pastor stopped mid-sermon and asked Eleanor to share a word. Totally unprepared, she stood to speak, but to this day doesn't know what she said. Nor do I, but God certainly anointed her. People flocked to the altar or knelt at their seats and in the aisles. Begging for our forgiveness, they released us with promise of their prayers.

The testing was over.

Shortly thereafter, OMS asked me to take Dale Mc-Clain's position. Dale, the regional director for eastern U.S., was needed to direct the Hong Kong field.

That same year Eleanor and I traveled to 13 different countries, covering South America and Haiti. We wanted to improve our knowledge of their language and culture, and observe their social and spiritual problems. During this trip I had a potent thought--why not start a full-scale crusade program?

What I witnessed in these deprived lands is what other men should experience. What better way than to actually go? That trip cost us most of our savings, but it was worth every penny. With renewed enthusiasm and much greater effectiveness, we plunged into our work.

In 1960 OMS reassigned me to headquarters--then located in California--to direct Men For Missions. Eleanor with great trepidation and no training, took over as editor of the MFM *Action* magazine. God so honored her diligence and stretched her abilities that she became editor of the OMS publication, *Outreach*--a position she has filled for 23 years.

This was a great period of growth for MFM. To follow up on the crusade program, in 1961 we began taking college kids from the west coast to several Mexican cities during their Christmas break.

While praying about how to involve people on a larger scale, I was reminded that for every serviceman in World War II, ten civilians worked to support him. Using that formula, MFM needed 2,000 laymen to bolster OMS's worldwide outreach.

With that goal in mind, we got started. The first year only seven people signed up for each of four crusades. We went to Haiti, Colombia, Ecuador, and Brazil. It was a small beginning, but the concept caught on and eventually grew into the massive program that exists today.

In 1964 Eleanor and I went to observe OMS's work in the Orient, just as we had done seven years before in South America. During our stay with Ron and Priscilla Harrington, OMS missionaries assigned to Hong Kong, we spent many hours praying and discussing possibilities for bringing groups across the Pacific Ocean. Sensing God's leading and acting on their counsel, we launched crusades to Japan, Korea, Hong Kong, Taiwan, Indonesia, and the Philippines, as well as other parts of the world.

My mind then turned to transportation expenses incurred by missionaries on furlough. John Boewe, a devout Christian printer, was also a pilot. On several weekends he and his wife flew Eleanor and me to Mexico to pass out medicine and hold services. John also began taking us to speaking assignments, thus cutting travel time. Largely because of John's participation and the impact of Eldon Turnidge, who was one of MFM's first presidents as well as a pilot, the Wings For Missions program was born. Soon other pilots saw the opportunity to use a hobby for God. Within a few years it was set up as an air service for missionaries on furlough. The late Harold Miller of Colorado directed the program and saw thousands of miles logged at great savings of time and funds for OMS.

Dwight Ferguson and I teamed up in 1969 to share the vision of Men For Missions with laymen of England, Ireland, Scotland, and Wales. During our Ireland stay, shooting and strife between the Catholics and Protestants created havoc. In spite of the problems this presented, God graciously brought together a small band of men who accepted the challenge of the Great Commission. Today many individuals and Men For Missions councils in the British Isles help OMS missionaries do a better job by participating in witness and work crusades.

Our Trucking For Missions program started in 1971 when Ken Milone, an Illinois farmer at the time, asked if I wanted to see his new truck. We walked outside and Ken said,

"The only thing that bothers me is that it will sit idle for half the year. I only need it at harvest time. I wish I could make it productive the rest of the year."

"Well, Ken, you could haul household goods from Greenwood to Miami or to the east and west coasts when missionaries leave for the fields."

God brought this willing layman to the right spot at the right time, giving birth to an idea that has eliminated hundreds of thousands of dollars in shipping costs for OMS ever since. I might add that Ken became an OMS missionary in 1975. Over the years as many as 30 trucks and twice as many drivers, have been available whenever needed. Due to highway regulations it became essential for MFM to purchase its own truck. Drivers are still donating their time, however, avoiding the high rates of commercial trucking. On many occasions commercial haulers work with us when empty or carrying a partial load.

The council program--groups of men who meet monthly to pray, plan programs to promote mission activities, and inspire others to get involved--began slowly but today over 100 councils meet regularly in the U.S. alone.

A few years after the birth of Men For Missions, the word spread to Canada. In 1967 a Canadian named W. L. Smith became president of the international cabinet. It was during this period that MFM membership in Canada began to grow. Councils formed and many Canadians joined crusade teams.

Before long, invitations came to present MFM to laymen in New Zealand, Australia, Korea, and Africa. God's networking system never ceases to amaze me. All that MFM is today came directly from Him. No man can take the credit. Through the years I've had the high privilege of simply being His conduit.

For example, I had been speaking in the eastern part of the United States and went to visit my brother-in-law, Hadrian Lechner, in New York State. He had purchased a new car and wanted to donate his older one to OMS. All that was needed was a few repairs, then I could start home, then in California.

To accomplish this I stopped to see Dick Witmer, an MFMer in Pennsylvania who was a car dealer. After looking the car over, he made a call to Howard Rowe, our mutual friend in Canada. We then left for lunch while the car was in the repair shop.

Upon our return I received the surprise of my life. Dick handed me the keys to a brand new car. God started it in New York with Hadrian Lechner and completed it in Pennsylvania, using Dick Witmer and a Canadian MFMer affectionately known as "Grandpa Rowe." You can imagine the excitement as I finished my activities and started across country. I had a new car, but more importantly, I had a new testimony to God's bountiful provision.

There are many "miracle" stories like that. I recall leaving the OMS office in Atlanta late one afternoon, heading for California. To get there for an important meeting, I needed to drive straight through. About midnight, however, I began to tire and was tempted to get a motel room. While asking the Lord to help with that decision, I stopped for fuel.

Since I'd often needed a ride when I was in the Navy, I made it a practice to accommodate hitchhiking seamen. So before leaving the station, I prayed, "Lord, I'll watch for your answer. If there's a sailor thumbing at the edge of town I'll pick him up and keep going. If not, I'll stop and get some sleep."

As I approached the outskirts of town, sure enough, there stood a sailor in full uniform. I stopped, we loaded his sea bag, and in a few minutes were on our way.

I began a conversation with my young friend by explaining how I happened to pick him up. His response was, "Sir, your story gives me goose bumps. I've been trying to catch a ride all day in civilian clothes. A few minutes ago I went behind a billboard and put on my uniform. As soon as I returned, you picked me up."

Building on this "coincidence," I asked him about his spiritual life. I soon had him reading from my Bible and talking about salvation. As we drove through the night he became a new creature in Christ. When we parted, I felt as though I were sending my son off to war, but I had the assurance he belonged to Christ.

A number of special incidents occurred during my travels overseas. While I was directing a witness crusade in the Orient, we boarded a plane to Seoul, Korea, at the Tokyo airport. We had been running late and didn't take time for devotions that morning. So I greeted my fellow plane passenger, secured my seatbelt, and took a New Testament from my pocket. After reading a chapter I bowed my head in prayer. When I opened my eyes, he was looking at me curiously.

"You're a Christian, aren't you?" he began.

"Yes, I am. Are you?"

"No, I'm a Buddhist."

I'd always wanted to talk frankly with a Buddhist, so I seized the opportunity. "If you'll tell me why you are a Buddhist," I said, "I'll tell you why I'm a Christian."

His story was predictable. He told me that his parents, grandparents, and great grandparents were all Buddhists. He had attended a Buddhist school and was taught to burn incense, toss wooden blocks into the air, and bow before the gods at the temple.

"That's why I'm a Buddhist," he announced proudly.

I responded by pointing out that there was a good deal of similarity in the way we acquired our religions. "I had grandparents who were Christians, and they encouraged my parents to be of like faith. Both of us were sent to schools associated with our religion. But that's not the reason I'm a Christian."

"You see," I continued, "even with all my training and encouragement I preferred to live a life crammed with sinful acts. I lied, cheated, and hurt people to satisfy my own desires. I was possessed with selfishness. Then I discovered the greatest miracle of all time. Jesus Christ died on the cross for the purpose of forgiving me of my sins. After that, He was raised from the dead and came to live His life all over again--but this time in me."

My friend's facial expression went from one of astonishment to one of interest. Then boldly I asked, "Where is Buddha today?"

"Why, he is dead."

"That is the all important difference. You worship a dead god. I worship a living One."

"If you can prove to me that Christ is alive, I will become a Christian," he declared. "I'd much rather worship a living God than a dead one."

I turned to John 20 and read from the Word how Mary Magdalene went to the tomb and saw that the stone had been rolled away, and how Peter and another disciple looked in and discovered that Jesus was gone. I read on, describing how Jesus had reappeared alive--first to Mary, then to his disciples who even touched the nail marks in His hands and the wound in His side. "Yes, Jesus was alive then and still is today," I told him.

At 30,000 feet, this Buddhist who wanted to worship a living God, confessed his sins and asked Jesus to enter his life. Five days later my new brother in Christ shared his testimony at our meeting of Korean businessmen in Seoul. They were moved to tears.

That incident brings to mind another which occurred in Bangkok, Thailand. I was leading a crusade that included the wife of a pastor. I saw her talking to one of our tour guides and suddenly burst into tears. When I approached her she said the young man was planning to become a monk. He was going to shave his head, go into isolation, and spend the next year in prayer to Buddha.

Making my way to the man, I prayed for guidance. I drew his attention to the tearful woman and explained her concern. "Friend," I reasoned, "she's crying because she knows your religious plan will lead you to eternal damnation. Why do you want to do this?"

"I want to find peace, and the life of a monk will provide that," he responded.

"Then why don't you consider the Prince of Peace, Jesus Christ?"

I told him about the sinful nature of man, how God sent His Son to rescue us, and that eternal life could be his for the asking. "Once you receive Jesus Christ as your Savior," I said, "you'll find the peace you are seeking."

He showed a genuine interest and listened intently. I could tell he was at a crossroad in his life. Within 30 minutes he asked Christ to forgive his sins and acknowledged Him as his Lord and Savior.

The pastor's wife was crying again--but this time with tears of joy. Although our time in Bangkok was short, we continued to work with this young man and within 24 hours had him registered in a Christian Bible School.

Then there was Ecuador. I had taken several crusades to that country and saw a population living in spiritual darkness, ensnared by saloons, houses of prostitution, and gambling dens.

When I presented the idea of a large group of MFMers impacting Ecuador for 30 days, the MFM cabinet enthusiastically set 1979 as the target date.

Known as "Penetration 79", our foray into Ecuador consisted of 37 dedicated soul-winners, each ready to put his hands and heart to the task. Landing at Simon Bolivar Airport in Guayaquil, we divided into three contingents: one headed south to Loja, the other north to Quito, and the third remaining in Guayaquil.

For the next month we concentrated on bringing the good news to thousands of Ecuadorians. Breaking into teams of two crusaders and an interpreter, we began walking the dusty streets. Knocking on doors, we introduced ourselves, shook hands, and presented the gospel. We were warmly received and often invited inside.

The Loja operation was a departure from the other two. These men had to prepare their own church before they could hold services. It was virtually a miracle. They built a platform and pulpit in an empty lot, and using the walls of adjacent buildings installed a roof of plastic sheeting. Electric lights were strung and posters advertising evening services nailed to hundreds of telephone poles. They even boosted attendance with a puppet show. The benches were filled each night with wiggling, excited youngsters, many remaining with the adults to hear the gospel message.

From carefully kept records this 30-day adventure produced 6,937 door-to-door visits, 11,404 people in attendance at   nightly services, and 1,037 definite decisions for Christ. Two new churches were also built from Penetration contributions--all a fitting climax to Men For Missions' 25th anniversary.

I also recall taking a large crusade to Saraguro, Ecuador. Dr. Bill Douce, a physician and OMS missionary, wanted to purchase a plot of ground for a clinic to serve the Saraguro Indians. The land cost more than OMS had available, so it appeared to be a lost cause. One of the fellows on the crusade suggested we go to the property site, form a circle around it, and pray--claiming it for God.

Dr. Douce appreciated his idea but said it would be a poor tactic. "If the landowners got wind of that," he explained, "they would raise the price."

Not to be denied, the layman countered with a different approach. "We'll still claim it. Let's send one man each hour to walk around the property and pray for its acquisition."

So we did, and within six months OMS owned the land. Not only that, I had the undisputable joy of laying the cornerstone for the clinic. What a day that was!

I was privileged to lay another cornerstone in Hong Kong during the refugee crisis. OMS was given land by the Hong Kong government to build a hospital for the refugees. So MFMers funded the entire structure and helped build it. A few years later the government decided there were too many hospitals and forced us to tear it down. MFM was again instrumental in raising money, this time to build a high school on the property. Today the school gives us a better opportunity to present the gospel, and we're reaching more people than ever before.

Another time God's direction brought tremendous results was in Allahabad, India. While on a work crusade there, I flew south to talk with Graham Houghton, an OMS missionary in India for years. Graham wanted to build a much-needed new seminary in Madras. With the tremendous lack of pastors and evangelists in that land, however, Graham felt he couldn't discontinue training classes in the old building during construction of the new one. I told him we'd trust the Lord to help us with a solution.

Leaving Graham, I headed back north to Allahabad, but had to change planes at a little town near Calcutta--a place I had never heard of. Upon deplaning I noticed a youngster look at me, then turn and run away as fast as he could. I remember thinking, "Did I scare that kid or something?"

Entering the terminal I received another of God's surprises. There was the boy, telling my good friends, Harold and Gloria Harrison, that "Uncle Harry" was outside. Harold was in the midst of telling his son he'd been in the sun too long, when he saw me. What a reunion that was.

Harold, a contractor, owned a construction firm in New Jersey and had just finished serving OMS as a consultant and construction engineer in Taiwan. After all the hugging, I said, "Man, has God ever put you in the right place. We need a contractor to help design a new seminary in Madras. Where are you heading?"

"Well, not there," Harold quipped jokingly. "We're on vacation." As usual the Lord had His man.

Harold went to Madras, looked at the property and made a proposal to keep the old structure intact until a new structure could be built around it--then the old one could be torn down. He flew to his home in New Jersey, put his own business in order, and returned to give God another period of his life. Directing teams of MFM work crusaders from Australia and the U.S., he made possible a very functional and attractive seminary.

If Harold hadn't been in that particular airport in India at that very hour, it's doubtful that OMS would be serving Christ in Madras as effectively as it is today. In a remote corner of the world, the need and the resource came together at a single point in time. No one but God could do that!

No one but God! Those four words contain the secret of the universe and eternity. It all belongs to Him, as does our salvation. Everyone who calls on the name of the Lord will be saved. But what about those who have not been told this good news?

Here in America the Lord's Word is available to everyone. Newspapers invite you to church, radio and television teach you the Word, billboards beckon you to city-wide revivals, and Christian friends urge you to repentance. But what about those who have not heard about Him?

If you'd like to help share the good news, you can--easily. Through MFM every farmer, tradesman, businessman, and professional can carry it--either directly by giving a simple witness on evangelism crusades, or indirectly by providing resources, skills, or abilities to missionaries at home and abroad. Nothing will bring you greater satisfaction.

3

Dean Baker

Some people think that success is reflected by such things as name recognition, the value of their estate, or the number of their subordinates. The misguided might even think spirituality can be measured by the amount of money they give their church. At times, mentioning the "correct" alma mater can achieve social, or even religious, recognition. Unfortunately the right position in business or the right church affiliation has become a coveted badge of value. Typically the Wall Street banker commands position while the Kansas farmer is ignored.

Men For Missions, to a great extent, is composed of "common men." Men who live in towns and villages many have never heard of. Who would guess that our strength lies in towns like Ekalaka, Montana; Bone Gap, Illinois; and Mountain City, Tennessee? Although God has given us outstanding members in major cities of the world, that's not where all the action is. Instead, most of our resources come from men living in remote areas of the country.

My friend Dean Baker is an interesting personality who fits that mold. Dean's farm faces a gravel road in an area of southern Illinois known as Little Egypt. Farming nearly 2,000 acres, he is a successful businessman so well known you can give directions by referring to the home in which he and his father were born.

Living in an isolated setting doesn't mean you can't have the latest farm machinery, however. Using it daily to make a living, Dean deviates from the norm by keeping it in immaculate condition. If you look closely you will find the dust blown out of the radiators and the metalwork waxed to a high gloss--every truck, tractor, and piece of machinery. His hobby? Collecting and restoring old tractors, of course.

This penchant for cleanliness is also a family characteristic. Barbara, his wife, and their grown children keep their homes, businesses, and vehicles in spotless condition. Dean's way of living carries over into his Christian life as well. He is a leader in his church, where over the years the Baker family has held virtually every office.

All of that, however, doesn't ensure spirituality--or even character, for that matter. Like Jonah and so many who came after him, Dean began his spiritual life by putting on his fastest shoes to run from the Lord. Ultimately he had to resolve this thorny problem. For some, Dean's story may be like looking into a mirror.

Golden Nuggets of God's Love

by Dean Baker

When hard times hit farmers during the depression, my father, Ivan Baker, decided he could keep us from starving by starting a community garage. It was a good idea because as a boy I helped him fix everything from hay-balers to tin lizzys. Like the kids of today, I didn't recognize the economic value of what I was learning. I certainly had no inclination to use those acquired skills in the Lord's service, either. I just liked being a "grease-monkey." It was more fun than farming, and that's all that mattered.

It was during those tough days that my mother, Carmen, used her well-grounded influence on Dad, and he eventually became a Christian. As a result I had good childhood experiences and even went to numerous church-sponsored revivals. I remember one as if it happened yesterday. I was 12 years old, and the preacher vividly described hell and its all-consuming, burning fire. That had a dramatic effect on me. The following night I went to the altar and became a Christian. I still recall the remarkable lifting of guilt. I also had my first exposure to missions during these formative years. I think that helped make me missions conscious and sensitive to MFM in later years.

Soon it was 1955, and I had just graduated from high school. Like most young men I set out to find a wife. Making that a major goal in my life, I began shopping around for the perfect girl. I soon fell head over heels in love with Barbara, an attractive, intelligent, and sensible farmer's daughter.

Barbara and I were married in the same Baptist church that her family had attended for years. Naturally she began persuading me to leave the Methodists and join her there. Her pastor surprised me one day when he made a colorful statement in her support. "When you get married you move your clothes to another house," he said, "so why not move to a new spiritual house as well?" Suddenly I had a wife, a different church, and a new life. I was aboard cloud nine.

A decade later, Barbara revealed that before we met she'd often prayed for a lifelong companion. What an impact that had on me. For the first time I realized that the Lord had blessed me, even though I had excluded Him from my plans. Those were youthful days, and I still felt comfortable with the illusion that I could do everything in my own power. Can you identify with that? I marveled at God's goodness as I considered the consequences of marrying the wrong girl.

I also entered the army in October of that year. I really didn't want to go, but I loved my country and I wasn't one to shirk my responsibilities. Barbara and I decided to make the best of it, and I was off to Korea.

The Korean war had just concluded but a lot of tension remained. I didn't see any fighting, but when the air-raid sirens screamed an alert we took it seriously and headed for cover. Most of my memories about Korea are negative, yet I can't blame anyone but myself. I was very lonely. I concentrated on my misery in being separated from Barbara, my parents, and southern Illinois. I also felt deflated because I saw no lasting value in my daily routine. My spare time (and we had a lot of it) was spent wishing I were home. If there was one thing I became good at, it was feeling sorry for myself.

I think the Lord used that time to teach me not to sit back and wait for good things to come my way. This truth came to life when, after returning home, I talked to a school buddy who had spent his military time in Japan. He told of working with children at several orphanages when he was off duty. It sounded so worthwhile and must have been very rewarding.

I felt embarrassed when he asked about my overseas duty. I could have done something helpful, too--but I didn't. I'm ashamed to say it never even entered my mind. I would have been willing, but I needed a leader.

In reconstructing those years I realize that if I would have met a man like J.B. Crouse I could have used him as a model and been productive. J.B., an OMS missionary, arrived in Korea about the same time I did. Today this Christian is known throughout Asia as a dynamic mover and shaker. What a leader to have patterned myself after.

I think another reason why the Lord let me walk through that lonely Korean valley was to make me sensitive to the "do, go, and give" mandate of MFM later. Especially the "do" and the "go." I've followed those simple directions for years now, and I recommend them from the bottom of my heart. I've never experienced that first pang of loneliness since I put my values in the right place. I don't wait for the good things in life to come to me; now I go after them. I also realize that I can be that leader lonely people search for. What an opportunity. And what a lesson He taught me. I am most grateful.

While I was in Korea, Barbara and I wrote constantly. In one letter she mentioned an offer by her father to let us rent a small tract of ground (at a very favorable price) and borrow some farm machinery to begin our nest egg. Upon my return, however, it seemed best that I work in my father's garage for a while rather than plunge into farming. That turned out to be a good move. With a year's savings in the bank we were able to acquire more ground, start investing in our own farm equipment, and begin our lifetime career of farming. By the early sixties we owned a fairly large farm.

We were good church-going folk involved in the things we thought appropriate to our lifestyle. Now that I look back on it, I think the Lord was preparing me for another lesson.

At one of our church meetings we met Everett Douce, brother of Dr. Bill Douce, an OMS missionary in Ecuador. I was quite impressed with Everett; he had a quality about him that exuded honesty and sincerity of purpose. Later I learned that he was going to Ecuador to help his brother build a clinic for the Saraguro Indians. Barbara and I felt we should help these men, so we gave a donation to their project. The money went through Men For Missions, which put us on the *Action* magazine mailing list. What an effect that little gift had on our future. We didn't know it, but we were about to embark on a new and exciting chapter in our lives.

I gave the *Action* a cursory examination while in the bathroom one day. Not particularly impressed, I pitched it away. In doing so, however, a message on the back cover grabbed my attention. My eyes riveted on its "Wanted" headline, then took in the intriguing message. Suddenly, and unexpectedly, I was bound to its call on my life.

Not asking for doctors, dentists, or evangelists, it pleaded for services I could perform--things like digging ditches, laying block, wiring buildings, and making cabinets. I felt the Lord was talking directly to me, commanding me to go. I had never experienced anything like this, but I was at ease with it and adapted quickly to the concept. I could actually go to a mission field, not to preach, but to do the things within my skills. What a tremendous opportunity to do something tangible--something I could look back on and feel good about.

But then I began to hesitate. Doubt crept in. Excuses flooded my mind. After all, I had a farm to attend to, a wife to look after, and we didn't have extra cash, either. Maybe I ought to stay right there and do my good works in southern Illinois. I laid the magazine down.

Forgetting about it, however, wasn't that easy. For four days I pondered the significance of the opportunity Men For Missions presented. I was all for it. But then uncertainty and self-designed pragmatism would creep into my mind, dilute my enthusiasm, and cause me to vacillate.

At this point in our lives Barbara and I didn't talk a great deal about spiritual matters. This lack of discussion seemed to magnify my conflict and frame it in the context of a wrestling match between me and God. The days turned into long hours of struggle. I became thoroughly preoccupied in this battle, so much that my attention to daily activities suffered. I began tossing at night, losing hours of sleep. But like

Jonah, my running and human resistance finally came to an end. Somehow I found the courage to take my stand and decided in favor of my Lord.

When I told Barbara of my decision, faithful to our relationship, she encouraged me to call Everett Douce and volunteer my services. The Lord was faithful, too. Everett responded to my inquiry by telling me that his brother, Dr. Bill Douce, was home from Ecuador. He happened to be standing by his side at that very moment.

Bill took the phone and asked if I could weld. Not ready for the speed at which the conversation was advancing and somewhat flabbergasted, I responded with a wacky answer I'll never forget. "Yes," I replied, "I'm a comfortable welder."

In short order I was in Ecuador on a month-long work crusade. Before I describe that experience, I must tell you that this first crusade started a series of events which really changed my life. It happened in a number of ways, but one of the most important aspects was how it eventually gave Barbara and me a whole new family. MFMers, for the most part, are actually as close to us as our blood relatives. The beauty of this wonderful relationship is that it continues to expand, even to this day. I've never belonged to another organization that offered me that.

But even with the support of my wife, the confidence of others, and knowing the will of my Lord, I began to feel inadequate as I prepared to go. My assignment was to build steel trusses for a clinic, and I began to doubt my ability. I quickly learned how hard Satan tries to discourage one. But he's ineffective when you wear the Lord's armor. Once I got started my butterflies left and everything went quite well.

A fellow crusader, Doyce Sheradon, cut angle irons while I did the welding. We toiled for days, enduring strange bugs, common mosquitos, insufficient supplies, and an uncanny number of equipment breakdowns. But in the end, a clinic superstructure stood tall.

It's standing the same way today, 24 years later. It's a monument--not to me and the others who worked on it--but to Christ's love. Knowing that from this place Christ's compassion has cascaded forth for all those years puts unbelievable joy in my heart. If I only could tear off a small portion of this joy and hand it to you! Well, we both know I can't. But, fortunately, the Lord provides a way in which you can experience your own. You don't have to have a diploma from Harvard or live on Million Dollar Lane. You just have to do what I did--quit running and believe in the do, go, and give mandate of Men For Missions.

While in Ecuador I met Jim and Lois Ogan, who were missionaries in Guayaquil at the time. Jim had heard of an unreached Indian tribe in the jungle. He wanted to make a survey trip, perhaps three or four days, to check on the possibilities for ministry there. When he asked Doyce and me if we wanted to go along, without much thought for our safety, we immediately accepted.

With provisions Lois prepared, we jumped into a muddy jeep and headed into the bush. After driving for several hours we arrived at a village on the edge of the jungle. Earlier Jim had contacted a villager who promised to meet us with pack mules for our trip into the jungle.

While we waited for the contact, Jim pointed out an Auca Indian carrying a handmade shotgun (the government had restricted Indians to single-shot weapons). "They're good with those guns," Jim said. "They keep them at their sides 24 hours a day." As the Auca slowly walked past, carefully looking us over, his suspicious glances were a perfect complement to his highly polished weapon. We were beginning to get a message.

Upon inquiry we learned that our arrival had been preceded by the murder of five missionaries* near this village. Needless to say, we grew increasingly apprehensive.

Jim realized that even if we found some mules, there was no safe place to leave the jeep. While we sat there, he began to pray. It was a new experience for Doyce and me; neither of us had ever prayed in a vehicle. But before long Jim sensed God's leading not to proceed, so we returned to Guayaquil.

---

*Jim Elliot, Nate Saint, Roger Youderian, Ed McCully, Peter Fleming.

Some time later Jim told us that the village had become the center of a tribal war. White men were excellent targets and were being killed. The risk of capture during skirmishes was also great. We thanked the Lord for Jim's sensitivity to His direction as well as His protection.

At the conclusion of the crusade, I returned to our small community in southern Illinois--never to be the same. With Ecuador on my mind and a new compassion in my heart, my life became intertwined with Men For Missions. Before long my friends and I formed an MFM council.

Our desire was to help missionaries any way we could. An opportunity came quicker than we expected. Word reached us that electrical power in Haiti was not adequate to keep the OMS radio station on the air. So we got together to rebuild the engine on a huge 120kva army surplus generator.

Working on this project really pulled our council together. We involved a lot of people, too--even non-Christians who caught our enthusiasm. The folks at Cummins Diesel helped by giving us a discount on parts. The job went on for weeks and we were often discouraged. But when we felt low, we prayed. Each time, the problem was solved and we were able to continue.

I remember the day we brought the generator out of the dimly lit garage, out into the sunlight for all to see. This was quite an event for our small community. Before sending it on to Haiti, however, we wanted a dedication service. To do it up right, our council sponsored a picnic on the Russell Koertge farm and asked Dr. Wesley Duewel, president of OMS at that time, to come and speak. In the meantime we loaded the massive, rebuilt generator on a flatbed truck and hauled it to the picnic grounds.

I'll never forget that moment. It was a brilliant Saturday afternoon when we helped Dr. Duewel climb onto the truck so everyone could see him. In his eloquent manner he dedicated the generator to the Lord, and prayed it would help bring many Haitians to Jesus. He then turned slowly, took a deep breath, and pushed the start button. The engine began cranking, then with a thunderous blast of black exhaust, surged to life.

All our aspirations and the Christian love and brotherhood we felt for the people in Haiti, changed from a dream to reality that day. A great roar of approval went up from the crowd; both men and children wept. The Holy Spirit made His presence among us very evident.

We delivered our gift to the Miami boat docks in a truck owned by a council brother. On the way back we bought a truckload of fruit and sold it to cover our transportation expenses. Once in Haiti, the generator brought consistent broadcasting to Radio 4VEH, the OMS station blanketing the Caribbean with the gospel. It also brought power to a medical, dental, and obstetric clinic, as well as a Bible school, the school for missionary kids, and a dozen or so missionary homes. The number of people who have been touched, even saved, because of this act of obedience is known only to God.

Our next big adventure began at an MFM retreat in Bone Gap, Illinois. Harry Burr, the MFM Executive Director at the time, had come with a dream. He wanted to take a work crusade to India--perhaps in a year or so. I listened intently. But India? I wasn't at all sure. A friend, halfway in jest, told Harry to put our names on the list. I didn't resist his draft, and in 1973, less than 18 months later, Barbara and I joined 12 other MFMers heading for the OMS seminary in Allahabad.

The sun was relentless in India, and beggars, like cattle clogging dusty roads, filled the streets. Most Indians are Hindus, and my heart bled when I saw their misguided devotion to countless gods. The impact of so many living out their lives in spiritual darkness profoundly affected me. How can we ever reach these multitudes, I wondered. Would the Lord show me a way?

Our seminary visit lasted a month and included work on a septic tank, library windows, and a suspended ceiling. We put in long hard days and after delicious evening meals were more than ready for bed.

In talking to the seminary students, Rudy Rabe, one of the OMS missionaries, found it difficult to explain the love we "wealthy" Americans had in our hearts for Jesus. Hinduism is deeply ingrained in their social and personal values, so they couldn't understand why "rich" whites would travel halfway around the world to improve their sewer. Only the low-caste and impoverished would work with their hands. When Rudy attempted to explain the phenomenon again, they said they understood. But I felt that in their hearts they rejected the possibility of such love.

I often wonder how things are in India today. I know that the OMS-related church plans to establish a thousand new churches by the year 2000. But the land is so vast, and there are millions of people. The Bible tells us, "He is not willing that any should perish," and I wonder what I can do to help save the millions that go into a Christless eternity each year. God taught me in Korea that saying "there's nothing I can do," is simply not acceptable. Although Barbara and I can't "go" to India every year, we "do" pray and "give" support to OMS in that part of the world, even to this day.

In 1978 Barbara and I went on an MFM Special Crusade, a Caribbean cruise. We had never attempted anything so out of the ordinary. We both wondered if it would be spiritually alive or just a time of vacation. Knowing MFM as we do, we should never have doubted. Spiritual activities abounded. We were in prayer or listening to inspiring messages by dynamic speakers each day and witnessed to the ship's crew through Bible studies and personal contact. We even had special church and school tours at each port-of-call, allowing us the opportunity to witness to a variety of groups.

Barbara and I have never had a desire to act in a leadership role on a crusade, preferring to leave that to MFM staff. So it was with some astonishment that Barbara and I were thrust into a supervising capacity. Our crusade directors, Warren and Velma Hardig, were called home suddenly because of a death in the family.

They asked if we would take over, probably because of our long association with MFM and our traveling experience. We wound up being responsible for fifty crusaders. What an eye opener that was. Although we didn't experience any serious misfortunes, we gained a lot of respect for crusade leaders. They certainly have their hands full--handling tickets, passports, reservations, and the like--yet they always seem to find time to solve a crusader's problems or provide much-needed information. I think it takes a special kind of person to do that.

The quality of the speakers was most impressive. Their messages seemed to zero in on the practical problems experienced by everyday Christians--even those of rural folk like Barbara and me. I'll never forget that cruise, not because of the fun and fellowship, but because I'm still applying many of the biblical principles I learned. It was the first time in my life that I was able to sit in one spot for two hours or more and enjoy every minute of it.

We experienced another spiritual blessing when we went on a crusade to the Far East in 1984. This time our hearts were broken for millions of Oriental idol worshipers. After observing and participating in much of the work OMS directs in that part of the world, we were impressed with the effectiveness of their missionaries.

I must admit the trip was somewhat exhausting as we loaded and unloaded suitcases in Korea, Japan, Hong Kong, Taiwan, Indonesia, and the Philippines. And then there were all those immigration and customs people we had to get by. But it was worth every aching muscle and every hour of lost sleep, to see and experience things that helped us put God's plan for the ages into better perspective. If you asked me, "Would you do it again?", my answer would be a resounding, "Yes!"

We even took a side trip into Red China, where it was like turning the hands of time back a hundred years. I could write a book comparing the quality of life in Red China to that of the West. But to put it in a nutshell, my impression is that we live in a world of color while they exist in one of black and white.

We crusaders were treated as special people by the nationals. We bemoaned the separation we saw between those who have economic security and the millions who do not. How deplorable that the average person wasn't even allowed in our hotel, and bicycles were the only transport of millions. When I multiply their economic plight by their spiritual darkness, my compassion for them deepens to the point of pain. I often wonder if I've begun to approach the outermost fringe of the hurt and compassion Christ feels for us. I suppose the pity and the sorrow I experienced does not lend adequate credibility to that example, but it does help me describe the weight of this dreadful situation and how I felt about it. My heart was violently torn.

Communism has tried to blot Christianity off the face of the globe, but its ring is hollow and it's no match for the Word of God. God may have allowed Communism to flourish for a period of time to neutralize many of the Oriental religions, but I think we're at the threshold of seeing Him turn that around. Today you can find Christians in almost every part of the world, and I'm glad I was able to see how OMS is working, day in and day out, to multiply that reality.

Back home once again, I found an excellent way to be of service to the Lord. My council brother, Ken Milone, had started an MFM trucking program, so I began assisting in its coordination. Like a duck takes to water, we rolled up our sleeves and went to work. We began by telling other MFMers about the transportation needs of missionaries moving their household goods to ports of embarkation. Not only were commercial movers expensive, the special handling our new trucking program gave their furnishings brought peace of mind and allowed them to concentrate on other details. We also moved supplies, such as tires donated by an Illinois dealer for missionary cars, to OMS headquarters in Greenwood, Indiana.

All this began with a single truck and driver. We were on the phone almost every day for a while--calling other MFM councils across the country, getting leads, and making contacts. We soon had a volunteer fleet of 60 trucks and 150 drivers. Ken and I acted as the dispatchers, sending them all over the United States and Canada, sometimes keeping three or four trucks on the road at once.

These men paid their own expenses and drove countless miles. I know we saved OMS thousands of dollars in rental truck costs, but more important, those MFMers got the opportunity to serve Christ in a tangible way. Many drivers would return excited about witnessing for Christ at truck stops and gas stations. I remember Jerry Kissinger, a 280-pound MFMer who couldn't relate his experiences without crying. What a program! Ken became an OMS missionary and moved away, so I continued by myself for the next eight years. MFM eventually bought their own truck, so the program was somewhat reduced. But it wasn't eliminated, and you might find a real challenge in this involvement if you have a truck and can donate your time. I certainly did.

As MFM Trucking Coordinator, I was considered "Associate Staff." This privileged me to attend semiannual cabinet meetings and really become part of the MFM team. January cabinet sessions are held in different cities each year, and once we met in Haiti. This helped me see the enormity of the OMS/MFM program and how much they accomplish for Christ. I'm so glad MFM had a place for me--a small-town boy with nothing to offer but a willing heart.

My most recent trip was a work crusade to help build a church in Mexico. But unknown to us, a major rift existed between the congregation and the contractor. The church was located in an extremely poor and run-down section of town, and the contractor was a tough talking, borderline alcoholic.

After unpacking, we drove to the church, only to discover a construction site with little evidence of activity. Materials, scaffolding, and debris blocked any meaningful work on our part. Next to this site we located a structure I can only describe as a chicken coop. The congregation had been meeting in this flimsy building for months. Thinking we were to arrive the next day, they had assembled to pray that the reluctant contractor would clear the site so we could work. For weeks they had been asking him to either resume construction or remove the obstructions. But he resisted to the point of threatening to sue if they touched his equipment. Intimidated and without legal counsel of their own, they were turning to the Lord for help as we arrived.

What tremendous results prayer can bring. Early the next morning, with no advance warning, the contractor and his crew removed the obstacles. We went to work on schedule.

Though the contractor was no longer involved with the project, he kept coming back to monitor our work. Gradually he began relating to us and learned that we were there because of our love for Christ. Here was a rough and tumble, hard-drinking construction man in the first stage of bowing to the Holy Spirit. What an example of God's power and grace. But it happens all the time. In fact, I have come to the point of expecting to see some of God's miracles every time I go on a crusade.

It's so satisfying to see the fruit of your witness and labor. That's one reason Men For Missions wants to get men on the field, to let them experience situations and events as I have. The men bring this witness home with them, too. Their lives are changed, and they have tremendous influence on other men.

I remember when we got a new petroleum delivery man for our farm. On his second delivery we struck up a conversation, and he said that he'd heard I worked on missionary cars. With that confirmed, he told me he'd changed the type of oil he used in his trucks and wondered if I could use the original oil for missionary vehicles. I gladly accepted the oil, which kept OMS cars on the road for months.

These are the kinds of treasures men reap by being part of MFM. Golden nuggets of God's love seem to drop into your pocket. It doesn't matter if you're on a crusade in Ecuador, attending an MFM pig roast in Montana, or participating in a council meeting in southern Illinois, the "good life" just seems to follow you everywhere. The reason, of course, is that the focus of all MFMers is not on themselves, but on Jesus Christ--and how they can best release their personal skills and abilities in practical, direct missionary involvement.

- Commentary -

You would think that a man with these events and experiences in his background would not only be good material for a book such as this, but would also have significant influence on family members. Dean does have that influence, but one of his more distant relatives, a real "doubting Thomas," still isn't buying. On more than one occasion this man has heard Dean describe his dangerous encounter in Ecuador, Voodooism in Haiti, Buddhism in the Orient, and Hinduism in India. But he always rejects the truth. In relating his experiences, Dean has never allowed himself to become the focal point of the story. Even so, after hearing of his exploits and ventures in over ten countries, this relative summed up his opinion of Dean's life and effort to serve Christ by simply saying, "Dean, I'm sorry, but I just don't believe it."

"Notice among yourselves, dear brothers, that few of you who follow Christ have big names or power or wealth. Instead God has deliberately chosen to use ideas the world considers foolish and of little worth in order to shame those people considered by the world wise and great" I Cor. 1:26-27 (Living Bible).

4

Chuck Merrill

*A*s I begin this chapter tears come to my eyes. I've worked with thousands of people in my lifetime, but the couple you are about to meet have humbled me more than any I've ever encountered. To describe Chuck and Nita Merrill as good Christians and productive members of MFM would be accurate, but such a description certainly would fall far short of its mark. You see, I believe their story ranks as one of the greatest ever told.

Let me tell you upfront that Chuck is blind--and has been for 30 years. But his testimony speaks for itself when he sings, "Thank you for the valleys that I walk through today." Singing, you see, is Chuck's way of serving. But it's not just the music, it's the circumstances propelling the lyrics that give meaning to the words.

Chuck was instantly blinded in an accident, causing Nita to raise nine children in a state of abject poverty. Often living on a half-pound of hamburger per meal, they would still leave the table with a full feeling--a fact which lends credibility to Nita's skill as a cook and homemaker.

Today they live in a small, modest farm home and their income is limited to Social Security. They travel in a well used van--their third. They wore out the others by driving over a half-million miles, all by faith, to sing in churches and at MFM functions. Nita guides Chuck as far as the restroom door at interstate rest parks, and they get their meals at fast food drive-throughs. Nita, who cuts through controversial issues with a doctrine sharpened by years of faithfulness, often says they live on Social Security and travel by faith--because they can't afford to do it the other way around.

Upon their return from a 15,000-mile singing tour across Canada and the United States (sleeping in 40 different beds), a neighbor asked, "What have you two been up to?" After Nita described their venture, the neighbor remarked, "I wouldn't do that for the world." Nita, with no hesitation, replied, "Neither would I."

Chuck and Nita probably have less financially than any couple associated with Men For Missions. Yet because of God's all-sufficient grace, they have accomplished far more than many wealthy people I know. If I could live two lives,

I would still not achieve for Jesus as much as they have. By giving us Chuck and Nita, God provides a stunning example of how He uses laymen--people just like you and me. These humble mortals, in faithfulness born out of tragedy, have encouraged thousands through their personal testimony and musical messages. Once you have read this chapter you, too, will join the growing group of those blessed by their dedication to Christ.

This is the heartbeat of Men For Missions. God wants men from all walks of life--from the poorest to the most affluent, from the laborer to the corporate president. There's room for everyone in God's house.

Accidentally Happy

by Chuck Merrill

Yes, I am blind, but don't feel sorry for me. I'm far happier than most folks you'll meet.

I was raised in a vaudeville family. My dad was a comedian and a singer; my mother sang and assisted with his act. I guess you might say I grew up backstage. Along with milk, I absorbed music and a lot of barbershop harmony. I got to be pretty good, too--even taught myself to play string bass. Of course I did it on a cello; I couldn't afford "the big one."

We knew a lot of important people in show business, and we were always trying to make a good contact. But there was one important person that we avoided--Jesus Christ. My folks sent me to Sunday school once in a while, but they never went along. Growing up I had everything on my mind except salvation.

I was playing bass with a dance band in Indianapolis just before World War II and enjoying every minute of it. Then my applecart was upset; I got my marching orders from Uncle Sam. The army sent me to upper New York State for basic training (which I certainly didn't care for). But I did love that part of the country. I had been told that the Adirondack Mountains were magnificent, so one weekend I decided to do some exploration. They were just as I had been told, all right, and I kept going back. Not because of the topography, however. You see, I also met an Adirondack girl. Less than a year later, Nita and I were married.

In December of 1943 the army sent me to Europe. Leaving Nita was disheartening and depressing. I promised myself that on my return I'd never leave her again. I saw more military action than I cared to but escaped without bullet holes or scratches. I often wondered why, because I left a lot of buddies over there.

Coming home was one of the happiest days of my life. I'll never forget catching my first glimpse of Nita. Her embrace brought me supreme happiness and contentment. I was home with my wonderful wife--never more to leave. If that weren't enough, I received another wonderful gift. I met my daughter for the first time. Nita and I had been married for over three years but spent only three months together before I left for Europe. What a day that was--what a homecoming! Everything was perfect.

We decided to set up housekeeping in Indiana where my parents lived, and that brought some unexpected surprises. I learned that my mother, brother, and his wife, had been converted and were now serving the Lord. Not too long after that, in a little country church, I saw my father go to the altar and accept Christ as his Savior and Lord.

All of this was quite impressive. I even went to the altar and knelt beside Dad, but I didn't make a commitment. As time passed I saw a tremendous change in him, but I still wasn't ready. I had places to go and people to see. I told everyone I wanted to go back to the Adirondacks where the hunting and fishing were good. In other words, I ran. I wanted the things of the world a lot more than I wanted God.

After four years in New York, things were beginning to look pretty good. We were buying a new house, had a nice car, and were expecting our fifth child. I had also worked my way up to a job I enjoyed very much. As a blaster in an open-pit iron mine, I handled explosives every day. The work was outdoors, interesting, and paid very well. To add icing to my cake, I had a little dance band for weekend performances.

Thursday, March 24, 1955 dawned a beautiful day. Northern New York winters are rugged--there's a lot of snow and budding leaves come late. But on this particular day a hint of spring filled the air. It was pay day, too. "How good life is," I thought, as I left the house for work.

About quitting time I began to clean the blasting shack. I was getting rid of (supposedly) non-volatile odds and ends by burning them--a standard procedure I had used many, many times. I remember standing about six feet from the fire, watching as the red-orange flames lazily consumed the waste products.

Suddenly a terrible blue-white blast, accompanied by a powerful concussion, hurled me to the ground! My ears rang, my heavy winter clothing was ripped and shredded, and I was completely disoriented. My confused mind shot "damage report" questions throughout my body. My nervous system demanded to know what had happened--what was going on.

Little by little my senses returned. Survival, that's it! Crawl away from the fire pit! Back off! Back off! My fingers dug into the frozen ground, my feet pushed. Then my mind brushed against reality--I couldn't see where to go.

I couldn't see.

As they loaded me onto a stretcher for the ambulance ride to the hospital, I remember crying inside, "O Lord! Why me? Why did this happen to me?"

Consciousness came and went. Bits and pieces join to form a loose recollection of the events and discoveries that followed--blood transfusions, intravenous feeding, oxygen tents, punctured ear drums, a broken jaw, missing teeth. I lost 30 pounds in the first week, and the prognosis was not good. They didn't expect me to live.

During my three-month hospital stay, I kept wondering how I would face life as a blind man. "How can I earn a living? How can I raise my family?" Images of blind people I had known burst into my thoughts--ever so vividly. I pictured myself with a sign on my back screaming, "I am blind," and--oh yes, holding a box full of pencils. Or perhaps I could stand on the corner and sing while strumming my bass fiddle. Should I get a monkey? It was so real I could hear the coins drop into my imaginary tin cup on the sidewalk. But all this, you see, I kept inside me.

I was too ashamed to turn to the Lord. Even though I had no answers for this awful turn of events, I couldn't bring myself to ask for help. I figured that somehow, someway, it would turn out all right. Then I would be back on top again--then I would serve the Lord.

I often wonder how I could have fooled myself like that. Perhaps I had some help from the great deceiver. My frustration became quite severe, eventually turning into depression. They put me on tranquilizers and prepared me for my first eye operation. It failed to help me. So did the next two. Each time my hopes would be high--only to be dashed on the rocks of despair. The operations merely fueled my depression.

My doctor finally sent me to the Manhattan Clinic in New York City where I was examined by a panel of twenty eye specialists. At least they gave it to me straight: "Charlie"--I'll never forget that doctor's voice--

"Charlie, you'll never see again."

The male nurse who accompanied me to Manhattan guided me out of the clinic. As we stood on the street corner waiting for the light, exhaust fumes filled my nostrils and the roar of a city bus assaulted my ears. One step forward and this nightmare could be over! I inched forward, then hesitated. The urge was almost irresistible. I tried to take the final step, but something held me back. I was restrained; my body was not mine to control. The roar subsided. I fell into a state of utter exhaustion.

Before long I developed ulcers, which became progressively worse. For the next 18 months I was in and out of a variety of hospitals. One day the doctor showed Nita my x-rays and pointed to a lesion as big as her hand. "I could operate and help him," he said, "but with his outlook on life, all my work would be in vain. He'd have this lesion replaced with another in six months, and we'd be right back where we started."

We moved back to Indiana. I thought it would help to be near my family again. Of course, it didn't. I was using tranquilizers heavily and started developing a Dr. Jekyll/Mr. Hyde syndrome. I acted one way in front of my family and another in front of friends. Within a few weeks my Indiana doctor decided to chance an operation. I had caused my wife to lead a miserable existence, been a poor father to our children, and was a bundle of nerves. With such an impossible situation, apparently the doctor felt I had little to lose.

The night before I entered the hospital, Nita was walking me to help relieve my misery. I hadn't realized how all this had affected her; I was far too busy thinking about myself. But that night Nita reached the end of her rope. Trying to cope with me and keep a family together (on almost nothing) had strained her to the breaking point. As we walked I heard a startling prayer: "Lord, either heal him or take him home."

The Lord had only one way to answer that prayer because spiritually I wasn't ready to "go home."

They took x-rays before surgery the next day, and the ulcer couldn't be found. I thought the doctor had made a mistake and told him so. He repeated the extensive battery of tests, only to confirm the fact that I had been healed. Just as Nita had asked. I was impressed, but somehow I twisted the significance of that miracle and put it in a box of my design.

Returning from the hospital I decided to show my gratitude to the Lord, all right, but wanted to do it *my* way. I walked into the little country church (where Dad was now a deacon) thinking, "I'll *play* my way back. I'll make God real proud of me."

For the next three years I accompanied all the congregational singing and special music. When the church doors were open, I was there--every time. Slowly, however, I discovered that church attendance wasn't the answer either.

Then came a visit to New York. I don't know why, but while talking to old friends I detected a contrast between those who knew Jesus as their personal Savior and those who didn't. The Lord opened my eyes to see--not blue skies or the smile of a child (as beautiful as those things are), but something even more beautiful--a Christ-filled life.

On the trip home scripture verses filled my mind. I hadn't paid much attention when Nita read from the Bible all those days, but some of it stuck. Now I fought to recall it. One verse really hit home: "I am the way, the truth, and the life. No man cometh to the Father but by me." Although not fully grasping the meaning, I came to the realization that somehow, someway, God had an answer for *me*.

When we got home I walked boldly to our medicine cabinet, removed all the medicine bottles, and pitched them in the wastebasket. Then I did the best thing I have ever done in my life. Dropping to my knees I prayed, "Lord, I've got to have help. I can't do this alone. I need you, Lord."

After that the darkness wasn't so bad. I wasn't so lonesome. Everything was better. I found an eternal Friend who would help me and never leave me. Nita and I put Jesus in the center of our lives, in the center of our home, in the center of our marriage. He began to make startling changes and, praise God, He's still making them.

I soon found that being blind does not excuse or exclude one from serving the Lord, either. Not long after my total commitment to Him, He allowed me to become part of a new musical group, the Prairie Grove Gospel Messengers. We sang at a variety of church functions, including Men For Missions. After several banquets and retreats, they asked us to pray about extending our music ministry to Colombia, South America.

What an opportunity. What a surprise. How good God is! We spent a week in Colombia, singing our hearts out. But instead of coming home with a satisfied feeling, we returned dejected. The need for Christian churches in that country is unfathomable. We pulled into our driveway determined to do something about it. Now I had something to do--something I could do for someone else. The Prairie Grove Gospel Messengers began singing at many of the MFM functions, and we soon found our way into the churches of MFMers. Before long we had received enough in offerings to be instrumental in erecting three churches in Colombia.

After that the singing group disbanded. Not dismayed, Nita and my youngest children joined me and my singing continued unabated. Since then we have raised enough money for a fourth church.

You know, I'm often asked, "If you could go back before the accident, would you?" My answer is always the same, "No." It's just that simple. I've been much happier as a blind man serving Christ than I ever was when sighted and lost."

5

Wally Yoder

*W*ally Yoder is God's man with a sense of humor. When introducing himself at an MFM function, for example, he might say, "I'm in the iron and steel business. My wife irons and I steal." This is usually enough to elicit an embarrassed groan from his delightful wife, Marilyn.

Wally retired recently from Yoder Manufacturing Co., a fabricating company consuming 90,000 pounds of steel a week for making travel-trailer chassis. Today he reconditions iron and steel antiques, but that's not what he's known for in Men For Missions.

Wally lets God use him to the fullest extent. A man with two rare qualities--vision and perseverance--Wally has sharpened my life and hundreds more just like me, because he's a man who makes things happen. In this case, the MFM work crusade program.

Wally can claim credit for channeling to OMS a sizeable portion of the man hours equivalent to one-hundred years of voluntary missionary service. And it didn't take a dime away from the OMS evangelism budget. In fact, the crusaders who made up this century of service also contributed several million dollars to OMS for field projects and missionary support.

Wally accomplished this by organizing work crusades. Not content to simply get a list of names and reserve airplane seats, Wally had them meet him at various airports for a briefing. Wally called this process, "seeing 'em off."

A little research showed that Wally saw a lot off, too. He flew to Toronto for four crusades, New York for 17, and saw 141 off at Miami. When I added a few other points of embarkation, I discovered Wally had briefed 180 crusades.

That's an impressive feat for one man and lends credibility to his election to the post of MFM cabinet president. But typical of Wally's humble personality, he says he didn't do a thing--"It was just Christ working through me."

Out of the Pew
and
Into the World

by Wally Yoder

I have to go way back to 1968 to tell this story--back to the time when Men For Missions was a small, fledgling group of men with a burning love for the Lord. They had a problem though--they were so understaffed they couldn't effectively accomplish their purpose.

I came to MFM by accident, just like a lot of other men, I suppose. A fellow from our community, Otto Beer, went to Haiti on an MFM work crusade, and when he returned showed us his slides. Well, I must say, that got me excited. I had never been to a Third World country, and I was appalled at what I saw and heard. Not only were their living conditions terribly inadequate, their spiritual life centered around Voodoo, a practice I found to be both hard to believe and repulsive. I knew that missionaries went to places like that, but until now their going just didn't seem important. This whole issue seemed to unfold in front of me--for the first time in 43 years.

Otto's enthusiasm was catching. He invited me to an MFM meeting, and I was so excited about my new-found discovery, I was the first one to arrive. I met some dynam-ic people, too. One couple was particularly impressive and helpful--Harry and Eleanor Burr. Later I learned that Harry was the MFM executive director. We talked about the purpose of Men For Missions and I felt their objectives really made sense. Why shouldn't the average guy have a direct involvement in the Great Commission? The more I thought about that, the more I was convinced that missions should be my avenue of service. I had realized years earlier that sitting in the pew every Sunday was not tapping my potential. Now I knew what to do about it.

As the evening wore on, I became more and more convinced that I had discovered a spiritual gold mine. They were discussing a work crusade to Haiti at the time, and I was so challenged I signed up to go. That was one of the best decisions I've ever made. I've been going on crusades ever since.

Haiti had a tremendous effect on me. I'll never forget my first impressions of that impoverished land and its indigent people. My mind drifts back to the time I rode an old (but colorfully decorated) bus through Port-au-Prince. I can still smell the foul odors and envision the poor, covered with newspapers as they slept in the streets. They used little charcoal fires to heat their food--mostly in tin cans. I had never seen anything like it. For the first time, I felt like the "ugly American" we hear so much about.

But then I realized they didn't understand the meaning of salvation, either. In fact, most of them had never even heard of Jesus Christ. They were caught up in Voodoo and all of its satanic rituals, superstitions, charms, and fetishes. Their witch doctors held "sacred" rites, cast spells, and practiced animal sacrifice. It was at that point that the importance of the missionary hit me square between the eyes. They had recognized years ago what I was just now seeing. I wanted to help them all I could. Then a warm feeling came over me as I considered where I was and what I was doing. That feeling told me I was in the Lord's will.

Do you know something else? I had been a Christian for 29 years and never been asked to share my testimony. Isn't that amazing? Harry Burr was leading our crusade and he asked me to tell the story of my conversion to a group of Haitian Christians. I was ashamed because I didn't even know how. I'm not blaming others; I guess that's a good example of how lightly I took my Christian faith.

I have no idea what I said. I'm sure it sounded awful, but I can tell you this--it made me stop and think. That night I took a hard look at my life. After I accepted the Lord in 1938, I conveniently restricted my Christian life to going to church and Sunday school--that's it. What did I have to tell people in my witness? Outside of accepting the Lord as my Savior, *nothing*. I was not contributing to anything of lasting value. I was a spectator, comfortably sitting back, watching as the spiritual battle between God and Satan raged on. "How easy the passive life is," I thought. I suppose the point I'm making is this: By the time you get on the plane to come home, if the Lord hasn't got a little corner of your heart you're an awful hard guy.

Another crusade to Haiti turned out to be one of the most interesting and rewarding I've ever experienced. Lowell "Buss" Rassi, a crusader who lives near me in northern Indiana, discovered that a water tower project had bogged down. Buss and I climbed a mountain behind the OMS compound at Cap-Haitien one Sunday afternoon and prayed about this practical need. Praying on that mountain made me sense Christ's presence in a way I had never before experienced. I know He was there with us--listening, encouraging, blessing us. Buss felt it, too. As we sat there, viewing God's handiwork in the lush mountains and blue skies, we decided to do something about it.

When we returned to the States, Buss and I investigated the mechanical aspects of building a water tower, then drew plans. We shipped construction material--forms, rebar, welding equipment, etc.--out of Miami and sent money to purchase sand and concrete. Then we went back to do the job. Two weeks later we had a 30,000-gallon water tank standing tall. This is what I mean when I say that sitting in the pew every Sunday doesn't tap a person's potential.

During the next few years I went on 18 crusades of all kinds--witness, work, evangelism, and special. My wife,

Marilyn, usually accompanied me; she's been as faithful as a wife can be. As I recall, she's been to Haiti twice, Brazil, Mainland China, Hong Kong, Taiwan, and the Philippines. She's come to love MFM as much as I do. I think one reason is because of the "family" relationship we've experienced. MFMers are really great people.

During this time I became quite familiar with MFM. I was surprised to discover that only three men were running the entire organization. They were literally buried in paper work, correspondence, and meetings. It was obvious that their ability to promote MFM was limited, so my thoughts turned to helping them. I discussed it with Buss, and we decided the best way to serve the Lord through MFM would be to involve new men in the work crusade program. Like two synchronous clocks, two hearts bound by a single purpose, we explored this fertile ground together. Soon our insight expanded, flowing from recruitment to coordination. If MFM could identify needs in the various OMS mission fields and establish the crusade dates and costs, we could recruit the men.

It was a clear, spring night in 1973 when we climbed into Buss's single-engine plane and flew from northern Indiana to MFM headquarters in Greenwood. That night we met with Howard Young, Tom Gold, and MFM director Harry Burr. We presented our ideas, and they were elated. Harry gave immediate approval and the "work crusade" program was officially underway. Harry said he had been praying for additional manpower and help in bringing new inspiration and growth to Men For Missions. But he didn't expect it to come from outside the OMS staff.

Everyone was excited over the new relationship between staff and volunteers--it was considered a new chapter in the life of MFM. But what would they call us? I think this was the most significant problem we had with the entire proposal; we even went to prayer over it. Finally it was decided to call us "associate staff." That was the beginning of a program which grew into a large contingent of volunteers--men who, with no more than a phone call, were ready to assist MFM in a number of ways. Today 33 men are in key associate staff positions. Their titles do not reflect the valuable service they give the Lord: Area Representative, Trucking Coordinator, Wings Coordinator, Professional Services Coordinator, Work Crusade Coordinator, and many more.

Buss and I really started from scratch. For instance, realizing we needed something to hand anyone showing interest, we designed the first crusade application. We also printed the first crusade schedule. In our initial year of operation we sent 11 crusades to several fields. When other OMS fields heard about our work, they wanted crusades, too. The second year we sent 18, the third year 21, and the fourth year 28. It really grew; we were into the 30s by the fifth year. Buss helped with the program until 1975, and through God's sustaining power I ran it alone until 1979--a total of seven years.

All this work presented a problem, however. I was so busy coordinating things, I didn't have time to go on a crusade myself. Nor did Buss. To recruit men we'd travel to MFM retreats and banquets all over the United States. I remember flying to St. Petersburg, Florida, to promote the work crusade program at a banquet, then flying home the next morning. Another time I drove to Iowa, attended a Saturday night banquet, turned around and was in church the next morning. Week after week was like that. It was our method of getting men interested in going on crusades and developing a name list. It worked quite well; in 18 months we had 1100 names on our list.

Sometimes we needed to put an emergency crusade together--and in a hurry. Headquarters would call unexpectedly: "Wally, we've got to send ten men to Colombia to repair storm damage. Can you make it happen in a week?" When I got this kind of signal I would ask the Lord to help me bring glory to His name. Then thumbing through my name file, I'd start calling the men listed under "Work Crusade, Colombia." It wouldn't be long before I'd have my crew assembled and ready to go. That might include extra suitcases packed with special tools and building materials. My goodness, I couldn't even estimate how many tons of supplies have been carried to the fields by crusaders, all at no cost to the mission.

Actually I just considered all this part of my job. But years later the awesomeness of the whole thing struck me.

Warren Hardig, by now the MFM executive director, described me as a "link-pin" between Christ and other men. The more I think of it, the more I see and appreciate his analogy. Often men would approach me later with, "Man, I'll never forget the night you called--it was like Jesus calling me to service." I really thank God for giving me that opportunity.

I was running my own company (Yoder Manufacturing) at that time and God blessed it in such a way that I was able to use its resources to pay the bills we ran up. As an example, my MFM phone calls averaged $200 a month for seven years. The company paid for the calls, applications, schedules, brochures, and postage. My wife and I averaged 48 hours a week for MFM and ran our business, too. We were totally involved and tried to make every second count.

A lot of that 48 hours was spent in seeing the crusades off. Once I put the team together I felt an obligation to meet them at the airport, brief them, and make certain they got on the plane without problems. It wouldn't be right to send someone halfway across the world without some sort of personal contact and instruction. I would leave my office on Friday afternoon, fly to the port of embarkation, and send crusades off--or meet returning crusades, all weekend. Those going to Colombia or Haiti would leave in the early afternoon; those going to Brazil would leave around eight p.m. Crusades to Ecuador often left at three a.m. so we would gather at midnight for the briefing. Sprinkled in between were crusades returning from the fields. Finally, pretty much exhausted, I'd head home on Sunday night.

I always enjoyed the recruiting aspect, but what I really liked was seeing them off. As I did, the name from my list became flesh and blood, and I've always liked making new friends. I loved talking to them, too--guys from all over the U.S. and Canada--linking them up and helping them get acquainted, telling them what to expect on the field and how to get through customs. That was the best time of my life.

However, it had a downside, too--waving goodbye. I wanted to go to the field with them each and every time. Many would call or write later though, or I would see them at another banquet. They would tell me what they learned, what they did, who they met, and almost invariably, how two weeks on the mission field changed their lives. That, my friend, was exciting to hear. I accepted it as a personal gift from Christ.

Take the case of Art Hoewing, a retired electrician who lives in southern Illinois. On Warren Hardig's recommendation, I called Art to see if he could go on a work crusade to Brazil. Warren told me he would probably be willing to go but might have trouble financing the trip. When I got him on the line, I told him about the crusade and asked if he would consider trusting the Lord for the funds.

"Well, Wally," he said, "that's already decided. This afternoon I got a $100 bill in the mail, with a note that said,

'You might need this.' It was signed: 'A friend.'"   With a school boy's enthusiasm, Art accepted the challenge to go.

I met him 30 days later in Miami. He was all excited. "Wally," he beamed, "the Lord raised the $1200 I needed in less than two weeks. Not only that, He gave me $98 dollars for spending money!"

Art was even more elated when he returned. "Wally, a big storm came across the Parana River and blew our power lines down just as we rolled in for two weeks of work. Everything was in a state of confusion. I told the crusaders that if anything ever goes wrong, the first person you should ask for advice is the Lord. So we prayed about it. Then I looked at the downed transformer and told the rest of the guys to string wire while I worked on it. If OMS waited for the Brazilian power company to fix it they might be without power for months. Anyway, by seven o'clock that night we had the power restored, and the crusaders were ready to work on their project. Now I know why you called me to go to Brazil; I had to be there to fix that transformer."

There was no question in Art's mind as to why he made that trip. The fascinating thing is--that sort of story is repeated time after time. It's just different faces in different places.

I didn't go on any crusades during those seven years, yet it was probably the most fulfilling time of my life. Unfortunately, however, running both the business and the MFM program affected my health and forced me to slow down. I turned over the reins of Work Crusade Coordinator to Ron Collins of Greenwood. He's been coordinating the program ever since. Of course I continued my involvement. I was placed in charge of the MFM field advisors and in 1985 began serving on the MFM cabinet.

As I look back over my life, I often wonder how I would have spent my time if I hadn't become involved with Men For Missions. I may have just burned it up, wasting day after day, year after year. Using my time constructively with MFM, however, has given me a warm, satisfied feeling--the kind you get when you know you're obeying the will of the Lord. Until that first MFM council meeting with Otto Beer I never thought about missions. I wasn't giving $10 a year to its support. As long as I knew the Lord and was the spiritual leader of my family my obligation was met--wasn't it?

Of course, the answer is no. The Lord used my first trip to the mission field to open my eyes to this. Once that occurred--well, look at the result. I discovered that the work of the layman is as important as the work of the missionary; it's just a different application of effort. I'm reminded of Romans 12:4: "Just as each of us has one body with many members, and these members do not all have the same function, so in Christ we who are many form one body, and each member belongs to all the others" (NIV).

MFM supplies just the right amount of organization to allow one part of the body to help another--laymen helping missionaries--each "laying a block" as they build Christ's church here on earth. My advice to you is to get to a field. I don't care which one, but go and get some exposure. It doesn't mean much until you see it, smell it, feel it, and experience it. It will break your heart, but if I had it to do all over again, I wouldn't change a thing. MFM is every man's opportunity to give personal obedience to the Great Commission--it's *your* opportunity.

6

Otto J. "Bud" McWethy

*W*hat is in a first impression? Sometimes everything. In the case of Otto McWethy, my initial impression could be summed up in one word--integrity. I say this because since he accepted Christ and found freedom from the claws of alcoholism, he has displayed the exemplary qualities of faithfulness, courage, and honor.

Over a casual lunch in a small, central Iowa farm town, my friend John McLaughlin made a first-rate suggestion. He described a man of principle named Otto McWethy, and suggested that he might be interested in Men For Missions.

Proposing that I contact him, he gave me his phone number and address from memory. I thought this spontaneous recital of information a little unusual until he said, "Otto goes by the name 'Bud'. He's my brother-in-law."

Following his lead, I wrote to Bud that I would be passing through his hometown of Fargo on a certain date and would like to meet him. Bud also responded by mail, his warm letter confirming our appointment.

The day before I was to arrive, I called Bud from the home of a long-time MFMer, Gideon Schlecht. Gideon lived in Medina, just a few miles from Fargo, and was also interested in meeting Bud. I was glad he wanted to go along because it's enthusiastic laymen like Gideon who sharpen MFM's cutting edge.

"Mr. McWethy, my name is Warren Hardig and I'm calling to confirm our twelve o'clock appointment for lunch tomorrow."

His response was conciliatory. "I'm sorry, but I'm scheduled to be at a surplus hardware show tomorrow."

"That's OK," I replied, "I'll try to see you the next time I'm in town."

"No," came his reply, "I'm a man of my word, and if I gave you an appointment I'll keep it." Even though I had written Bud months earlier, I'm certain he wondered exactly what I wanted and was probably thinking he was in for an afternoon of high-pressure solicitation.

The next day Gideon and Bob Sutherland, furloughing OMS missionary to South America, accompanied me to the luncheon. On the way I learned that Bud, a 35-year-old entrepreneur, owned Mac's, Inc., a Fargo-based distributor of variety hardware. His business expertise enabled him to open a chain of additional stores in North and South Dakota as well as in Minnesota. After warm introductions, we left his enormous Fargo headquarters for lunch.

Once seated, Bud politely asked what I wanted of him. Although having lunch with the owner of a merchandising conglomerate can be intimidating, I had prepared myself through prayer. I began by relating the history and purpose of OMS and MFM, and concluded by trying to interest Bud in becoming involved. I could tell he was listening to my words but their impact seemed to have little effect. He appeared to be waiting for the capstone through which he could link my suggestion to his perception of serving Christ. Somehow I failed to breach that important chasm.

Bob Sutherland, who was senior to me as a missionary, attempted to rescue the situation by telling of his work in Colombia. It was easy to tell, however, that we weren't making progress. Then the Holy Spirit prompted me to ask Gideon to relate his experiences while on a crusade to Brazil. Gideon, a humble North Dakota cattle rancher, began by explaining he had stepped out in faith in order to give personal obedience to the Great Commission. However, as he did, one of his cows died--then another. These were his best cows and their deaths resulted in serious financial setback. Thoughts of canceling his crusade reservation began to fill his mind.

Gideon told of his struggle to overcome this newly imposed emotion--an intense desire to "stay home and tend to business." Counteracting that influence, however, was the potency of a spiritual nudge--an impression instructing him to go. The issue was eventually resolved in the quietness of his daily devotional time. God, in his simple, loving way, humbled Gideon by prompting, "Who owns those cows, anyway?"

Gideon then described an evangelistic service in Brazil where 15 undernourished youngsters gave their lives to Christ in a small, adobe church. As he did, he began to weep. Sketching a scene which depicted these deprived teenagers thirsting for love, then colorfully painting the joy they expressed when they found it in Christ, Gideon took Bud's attention prisoner. I could see glory come across his face. It was then the capstone was inserted and Proverbs 27:17 played out:

> As iron sharpens iron,
> so one man sharpens another.

As a result of that luncheon, Bud began his adventure with MFM by going on work crusades to Colombia. He even made his company trucks available to the MFM Trucking

Program and has been a valuable, productive MFMer ever since. I have no doubt that Bud was used by the Lord to sharpen my life. I had tried to influence him through logic, but failed. Gideon, on the other hand, spoke from the heart, allowing the Holy Spirit to redirect Bud's life. One heart speaking to another--one laymen sharpening another and rousing him to commitment. I will never forget that lesson and the wonderful work for Christ that Bud's decision brought to Men For Missions.

The Bottomless Bottle

by Otto J. "Bud" McWethy

To relate my life's experiences adequately and characterize my relationship with the Lord, I feel obliged to describe another relationship--one with my earthly father. In my youth Dad was a hard worker and always provided the basic necessities of life, but that's about all. At an early age he rebelled against anything religious and did not provide spiritual leadership in our home. I suppose I could label both of my parents as "holy day" people, folks who were preoccupied with life's compelling activities and only attended church on Christmas and Easter.

Strangely enough, my father had an oblique slant to his philosophy of life. Even though he felt religion wasn't necessary in his life, he decided that my older sister and I should "properly receive this formal indoctrination." He required, therefore, that we attend Sunday school at a Lutheran church and go through their confirmation process. Dutifully, I did, and in the eyes of the church stepped from child to adult at age 15.

I admired my father in some ways. Although he only completed one year of college, he was gifted with a sharp, quick mind and exceptionally accomplished in mathematics and creative thinking. He was also an excellent carpenter, mechanic, and electrician, possessing tremendous physical strength. I tried often to please him, but my skills matched none of his.

Unfortunately, the only things my father and I had in common were our hot tempers and love of alcohol. Dad was an alcoholic for many years, and I have distinct memories of his tirades and long absences from our home. Regrettably, the scenes of those days are hauntingly etched in my mind. Somehow my brave mother suffered through those troubling times, although I know she must have been near her wits' end.

I'm certain Dad acted as a role model, albeit a negative one, because I started drinking while in high school. In the beginning I was able to hide it, but as time went on that became more and more difficult. Becoming quite open with my "escape mechanism", I sometimes wonder how I ever graduated. It got to the point that I almost daily ran the risk of being caught and expelled. Naturally my grades and social life nose-dived. It would be many years before I came to grips with this problem and the terrible waste that lies in the bottom of a bottle.

My first meaningful exposure to Christ also came during my high school years, not as a result of my confirmation, but during an evangelistic crusade held at a Fargo high school. I can't remember why I went, but my sister and a friend-- not my parents--were my companions. When the invitation was given I recall a spiritual struggle within me. I gathered enough willpower to go forward, and someone I didn't even know prayed with me. I verbally committed my life to Christ, but it was a very weak commitment. What it did, however, was present me with two new problems. One I solved quickly, but the second was far more consequential and lasted much, much longer.

Walking home that night I was filled with mixed emotions. I felt good about what I had done but fretted over sharing the experience with my parents. After wrestling with the issue for several blocks and fearing their reaction, I resolved problem number one. I decided to remain quiet and say nothing. The problem with alcohol would have to wait.

Two weeks after graduation I joined the U.S. Army. Once I completed basic training, I was sent to Korea for 13 months, then to Germany for an additional 28 months. During my years of service I often thought about God and my "commitment". I even kept my King James Bible displayed on my foot locker. Why? I'm not certain. Perhaps for good luck, because spiritually it was pure hypocrisy. I was giving my entire allegiance to alcohol, not to God. My desire was simply to get through the day so I could relax with booze and buddies in the evening--the only part of the day I looked forward to. God must wait a little longer.

From the moment I went forward at the evangelistic crusade in Fargo to the moment I was discharged from the service, I prayed the words, "God, help me cut down on my drinking." I was in a constant turmoil. I knew the way to salvation and I wanted God to have his rightful place in my life, but if I surrendered to Him I knew I would have to give up drinking, my immorality, and my friends. The price was still too high.

I remember two men serving alongside me who made a different decision. They had gentle spirits and read their Bibles openly. I joined my buddies in poking fun at them and making light of their beliefs, but inwardly I desperately wanted what they had. In retrospect I believe God may have placed them there to remind me that peace and joy do not come from a bottle, but from a relationship with Him.

Since my father and I did not have a close relationship, I was not only surprised to receive a letter from him, I was astounded at its content. Dad related how he and Mom had received Jesus Christ as their personal Savior and were born again. I read it and read it again, unable to believe the words on that paper. I was truly elated over the news--yet it underscored my own failures and seemed to create more complexities for me.

I had a "new" Dad and a very excited mother. God had truly transformed my folks, but the changes were most evident in Dad. They had settled into an Evangelical Free Church, were attending, and reading the Bible regularly. I was really happy for them; but my love of the bottle remained firm.

Returning to Fargo in 1963, I went to work for my father in the hardware department of a discount store owned by him and my uncle. My life of corruption and immorality, however, continued at break-neck speed. I knew the gospel. I knew that Christ had died to take away the sins of the world and that anyone placing their trust in Him would be forgiven. I also knew that doing so meant I would have a new master. The Holy Spirit pulled at my heart, telling me that my lifestyle was abhorrent to God. But I resisted and drank more than ever to salve my wounds. My spiritual battle seemed endless.

I was 26 years old when I met the girl of my dreams. I knew God had picked Mary just for me and I fell madly in love. Since I hid the extent of my alcoholism, our courtship was perfect, our compatibility excellent. Together we were enjoying life's magical moments. I asked her to marry me and was incredibly elated when she accepted. Mary was brought up as a Catholic and, of course, I had a Lutheran background. Since my parents were now with the Evangelical Free Church, we decided to get married there. The same pastor who led my folks to Christ, Stan Nelson, would marry us.

Several weeks before the wedding, Stan made arrangements to meet us over coffee. After the usual niceties, Stan got down to business. His policy was simple. He would not marry us unless we were both true believers in Jesus Christ. This caught me off guard, as I subconsciously questioned my position in Christ. My mind flashed back to my youth--I was going forward at the high school altar call. Suddenly those thoughts were overshadowed by images of wild drinking bouts and shameful escapades. How was I going to handle this? Beads of perspiration broke out on my forehead. I sensed a violent clash deep within my heart.

I felt as though Stan were reading me like a book. I hesitated then stammered through the motions of responding to his invitation to repent and accept Christ. This was a turbulent experience for me. Apparently I was fooling Mary and Stan, but I knew that Christ heard every lie. By the time Stan left I was physically exhausted and spiritually devastated. But I got what I wanted; he agreed to marry us.

Mary and I had everything a young couple could want, except happiness, as my drinking quickly came between us. When we were blessed with a bouncing baby boy I thought things would be better, but they grew worse. Alcohol was more important to me than Mary, then it became more important than my newborn son. It ruled my life. I needed it, loved it, even worshiped it. I would never have admitted it, but in the depths of my psyche I felt alcohol was the god of sustenance and pleasure--the god of choice.

About that time we got a new pastor, Dick Hess, whose hobby was building mechanical things and tinkering. He often came to our surplus store looking for odds and ends for his projects, and we became good friends. I even started going to church more, but it was not life-changing. Still, he was a good influence on me.

Then on top of my drinking and my marriage situation, a business problem developed. I had always had good relations with the people who worked for me at the surplus store, but even that began to sour. Trying to supervise employees in an environment of conflict plunged me into a period of frustration. The tension mounted to the point of hemorrhage. One day when things were at a critical state, Dick came bounding into the store. "How's it going, Bud?" he asked.

"It's the pits," I responded. Suddenly the floodgates restraining my stress broke open, and I engulfed him with my management problem.

Dick listened intently, then in his down-home manner said, "Bud, since you're a Christian, you can take these things to the Lord and He will help you." His statement threw me into a tailspin. Though I tried not to show it, I was shaken to my core. I was expecting to receive personnel advice, not spiritual advice. But with that simple statement Dick made me confront my affliction--a spiritual maleficence.

That evening, choked with heartfelt regret, I threw myself across my bed. Weeping, I confessed to being a sinner in need of repentance and asked Jesus for forgiveness. I had been running from Him too long. I admitted I was at a fork in the road, and audibly rejected Satan's path in favor of the road to salvation. Between sobbing gasps for air, I begged Jesus to take control of my life, free me from the chains of alcoholism, restore my relationship with my wife, and indwell me with the Holy Spirit. I prayed long and hard, never wanting something that much in my life. I know He heard me because when I rose from my bed I felt a peace I had never known. His miracle touch immediately removed my agonizing and continuous craving for alcohol. His inward process of spiritual transformation continues to this day.

In His marvelous grace He even led Mary and me into the first home Bible study our church had. It was led by Dick Hess, who was very patient with me, because I tied him up for hours asking questions. How very rewarding the experience was. I could distinctly feel the Holy Spirit's new and prominent influence. My homelife became a virtual joy as I abstained from alcohol. Mary and I still are involved in the home Bible study program.

A few years later, I believe it was in 1976, my sister and brother-in-law, John and Mary McLaughlin, went on a Men For Missions special crusade to Haiti. They visited us in Fargo a few weeks later and shared the excitement of this spiritual adventure. I have to admit that my wife and I found the idea of going on a crusade very appealing. I was so tied down in my business, however, that I didn't think I should take the time. Nevertheless, God had planted the seed and it wasn't long before Warren Hardig, the Executive Director of Men For Missions, came along to water it.

By the grace of our wonderful Lord, my surplus hardware business has grown beyond all expectations. When I met Warren and a couple of his associates for lunch, my friend and general manager, Marvin Faul, joined us.

As our conversations progressed, Marvin and I began to develop enthusiasm for missions and the work performed by Christian laymen through MFM. I think the Holy Spirit used a heartrending story told by one of the laymen accompanying Warren to sensitize me to the need for missions. Once I understood the underlying reason for their work, compassion filled my heart and I was ready to give my all.

Surely this man was sent by God, and this was the work He wanted me to do.

Six weeks later I got a call from MFM describing a desperate need for construction help at the OMS seminary in Medellin, Colombia. Marvin and I prayed about this and both felt the Holy Spirit leading us to go. We dropped what we were doing, got our shots (required at that time), flew to Chicago to get our passports, then met the rest of the crusade at the Miami airport--all in three days. After a briefing and prayer, we boarded an Avianca flight for Colombia.

That was the first of five trips to Colombia and many soul-satisfying experiences. The Lord even spoke to me through some of the events I encountered in Colombia. I remember one in particular. Leaving Puerto Berrio in a motorboat, then transferring to a dugout canoe, we met with a small group of believers deep within the jungle. When we arrived these dear people gave us their absolute best for dinner--a baked potato and some salt. We sang gospel songs and had a short devotion, but it was the joy we saw on their faces and the generosity they extended that told us Christ lived here, too.

Perhaps my most vivid and powerful experience, however, revolved around my own past. At sunset one day we were in a small Colombian town passing out tracts. It was then I saw an old woman dressed in black, sitting on the ground in a darkened doorway. She was bent over, sitting with her hands on her knees, her head bowed. Her face conveyed total emptiness and despair. To me, in the waning light, her silhouette represented the darkness of sin--a darkness that covers the world. How dismal and bleak it is without Christ. Then, in an instant, I saw myself sitting there. It became even darker, but I saw the same expression of hopelessness on my face, and in my hand--a bottle.

The vision shocked me at first, but then I understood its meaning--a reminder of my rescue from the demonic pit, and the value of the light by which I now walk. Its message was clear--be alert and sensitive to the leading of the Holy Spirit and my walk with Christ will be sustained.

Today my sons, Chuck and Mike, are the second generation of McWethys going on MFM crusades. Both boys have been to Haiti and the Lord is providing them with their own wonderful experiences. In fact, Chuck was even baptized at the OMS compound in Haiti. I have a feeling that the McWethy line will be associated with MFM for many generations to come.

It is not possible for me to express the love I have for Jesus Christ and my gratitude for what He has done for me. I can best approach that impossible task, however, by relating my story to others--a story that began at that luncheon with Gideon and Warren. One man sharpened my life by telling of God's miraculous intervention and His saving grace. Iron sharpening iron--allowing me to see the character of Christ being played out in another man's life.

Later, my friend Warren told me that my subsequent actions sharpened his life. Certainly, God's Word is consistent and perpetual.

7

Wade Armstrong

*W*hen I think of Wade Armstrong my mind drifts to southern Texas and the rugged, wind-swept face of a man with irresistible charm and appeal. A man whose gentle, amiable eyes counteract his weathered features, Wade is a true Texan--hardy as the day is long, yet filled with love and charity for his fellow man.

Wade, like me, was a "good church member" for a number of years before he surrendered his life to Christ. His conversion came while he was on an MFM crusade in

Ecuador--a place far from Texas and his familiar surround-ings, but the exact spot where God wanted him.

God did a great work in Wade's heart that day. He took the raw material of Wade's past life and shaped it into a trusted servant. You can see that godly act reflected in the twinkle of Wade's eye as he contemplates his next undertak-ing for Christ. His engaging charisma--molded from his craggy features, his cheerful nature, and his new spirit--is a marvelous gift from God.

It's for these reasons I've given Wade the informal title of "Mr. Hospitality". As he circulates throughout the United States attending cabinet meetings, visiting councils, and helping with MFM farming programs, Wade is Christ's ambassador *par excellence.*

Look What Christ Did

by Wade Armstrong

Does your memory drift back to your childhood as easily as mine does? I have delightful visions of those early days. There was winter, with a nip in the air and the crunch of

frosted goldenrod underfoot. Then summer came, with the
sun heating the earth just to warm my bare feet. I remember the endless porch with its line of rocking chairs, and the
aroma of country-fried chicken drifting across the meadow.
Mother was a superb cook. So when we played outside, my
brother and three sisters and I took turns peeking in the
window to watch her prepare Sunday dinner. I can still see
that honey-sweetened whole grain bread, pickled beets,
steaming bowls of corn, and thick chicken gravy.

It's not that we always had such mouthwatering meals on
Sunday. You see, my father was in charge of securing
preachers for our community church, so he often asked them
to stay at our home while in town. Father was a strong, sun-
baked farmer who always put his family first. To be the
good provider he was, he worked in the fields long past dusk,
coming home only when he could no longer see to work.
For that reason most of my memories are of my mother.

We lived in the country near Sulphur Springs, Texas,
and I recall Mother's important role as the community nurse.
Although doctors made house calls in those days, winter
snows and rutted dirt roads prevented them from getting to
many country homes. Mother was always ready to help out
in those trying times. I can still remember her wrapping her
feet, bundling up in two overcoats, and with a bushel of
canned goods making her way to an ailing neighbor's home.
She might be gone for a week at a time, sitting up with the

sick, nursing them back to health, or just helping with their chores.

I only mention this because I enjoy visiting those years of contentment. Maybe it was because of my parents' love and that simple, yet bountiful country lifestyle that I came to like and value people so much. It seems I've always had an authentic appreciation and concern for people. But it wasn't until much later in life that I was able to blend that feeling with something of spiritual value.

I loved high school. Lean and mean, I filled most of my time playing baseball and basketball. During my junior year as a rough and tumble football player, I made All-State. But teamwork was my real hallmark. It seemed so easy; the players willingly followed my lead, and we moved through our plays like a well-oiled machine. "If being an adult is going to be this simple," I told myself, "the world is my oyster."

So I proceeded to the next, and most predictable, step in any young man's life--getting married. I met Sybil in high school while working for her father. That was some job. I worked an old-fashioned, mule-powered hay press out in the fields. It was hot, dry, and dusty. In fact, it was the most boring thing I had ever done in my life. I think I would have exploded with frustration if Sybil hadn't come into the picture. We caught each other's eye, and before long she was bringing me lemonade. Well, one thing led to another, and sure enough, I married the boss's daughter.

Married, and just out of high school, I joined the air force. This was during World War II, and I was immediately sent to Italy. Working in an airport control tower, I must have helped land thousands of B-24 bombers in the 16 months I was overseas. It was good duty, but I surely was glad when the war ended and I could return to Sybil. After a jubilant reunion, I knew it was time to get a job and settle down. I first worked at a clothing store but didn't like that so I moved on to a shoe store. It wasn't much better, but without a college degree and in competition with thousands of young men returning from service, the pickings were slim. I eventually wound up with Lance, a nationally known cookie company. Working hard and relying upon my communication skills and ability to make friends, I was soon promoted to branch manager. Success was in the air, and I began a 27-year relationship with a great employer.

By this time Sybil and I had two of our five children. We wanted to set a good example and give them high standards, so our thoughts turned to church. We were living in Waco, Texas, and after scouring the city we decided to join the newest church in town, the First United Methodist. Sybil was very serious about this church business--perhaps because of the children, I don't know. But she always made certain our family was in Sunday school and church every week.

As I look back on things I really praise God for Sybil. She was the spiritual leader in our home for many, many years. If she had not been, I know our children would have suffered. I have to admit that I was one of those "Sunday Christians" you hear about. I made my appearance in church every Sunday, but the weekdays were mine, and I wasn't worrying about spiritual matters. My concerns were about my work and how I could get ahead financially. It's ironic, too, because even with my apathetic attitude, I became president of our Sunday school program and eventually became a church board member. Of course my church activity was fired by my desire to be accepted socially. With my easy-going nature that was not difficult at all.

This lifestyle continued for several years, then in 1978 we received a letter from our pastor, Richard (Dick) Freeman. He invited us to a special Men For Missions meeting he was sponsoring. The guest speaker was a fellow from Illinois named Warren Hardig, and he was to talk about mission work. Personally, I could have found other things to do. But Sybil, with her natural affinity for the spiritual side of life, was all excited. Her curt, "We're *going*, Wade", quickly settled the issue.

As Warren described OMS International and Men For Missions, my mind wandered like that of a seven-year-old on his way home from school. I thought about problems at work, things I had to do at home, and where I might go next weekend. I considered taxes, local government, and world affairs, but solving none of them, recycled the mishmash in my mind until I was numb. When my concentration came back to the meeting for an instant, I asked myself, "What in the world am I doing here? This guy just wants some money."

Warren droned on as my meager attention vacillated between little and none. On one occasion I remember thinking, "Maybe if I give him five or ten dollars right after he's finished I can slip out of here unnoticed and not get trapped."

I don't know if Warren was aware of my disinterest, but it seemed he was looking right at me. That made me a little uncomfortable so I started listening to him, mainly for self-protection. I was afraid he might ask me a question. Before long, however, my negative attitude began to change. He was discussing the possibility of our church starting a Men For Missions Council, and I became mildly interested--if for no other reason than to feed my penchant for group activities.

When Warren concluded they served refreshments. Sybil and I went to the brochure table, and the first one she picked up advertised a witness crusade leaving on July 19. "Look at this," she said, "a crusade leaving for Ecuador on the day my vacation starts. We could go!"

"Good heavens," I thought, "Ecuador? Like in South America?"

Sybil was an officer in the trust department of a local bank at that time and was locked in on her vacation schedule. Of all the days in the year, I couldn't believe how the crusade date and her vacation coincided like that. I had retired from Lance and was now an independent contractor with considerable freedom, so I could hardly argue that point. What's more, Sybil's brother and sister-in-law, Mike and Bonnie Shrode, had become missionaries with OMS recently and were preparing to go to Ecuador. In the twinkling of an eye, the die was cast; Sybil was ready to go.

I must admit I was warming to the idea. Mike and Bonnie have children, and I had often wondered what they were getting themselves into. My concern was from a financial point of view; Mike had left a high-paying job with Exxon Oil and Bonnie was making good money as a school-teacher. It would be interesting to visit them and see what caused them to leave an excellent future in the United States for the Ecuadorian jungle. Arriving home we continued discussing it. But our conversations were about getting shots and passports, not whether or not we should go. We mailed our application to MFM the next day.

Strangely enough, we were turned down. The crusade was already full, and we were relegated to a waiting list. We waited for weeks, and the longer I was denied permission, the more I wanted to go. Finally I decided we would pray about it. "Lord, if You want us on this crusade, please open the doors and allow us to go." All of a sudden I realized what I was saying. Only days before I was adamantly opposed to what I was now praying for. Was the Lord speaking to me? Confirmation of this new relationship with the Lord came a few days later. A letter informed us that MFM had a cancellation. We were on our way to Ecuador.

I suppose the first crusade anyone goes on is a real eye-opener. It certainly was for me, and I didn't have any idea what to expect. Being uprooted from my favorite pew and thrust into a herd of unknown Christians set on climbing around in the Andes was somewhat disquieting, to say the least. But I soon began to learn things from this impassioned group of advocates.

When we arrived at our rendezvous point in Miami, I discovered there were 27 others going on this crusade. But the significance of the whole thing didn't lie in their number, it was in their relationship with Christ. I was really startled when some of these strangers invited me to join a prayer circle and asked God to help us witness in a manner that would bring glory to His Son, Jesus Christ. It wasn't their prayer that was so exceptional, it was the setting--right in the middle of the Miami airport with hundreds of people walking by. It seemed that every eye in Florida was on us, but that didn't affect their determination to commune with God. "Wow", I thought, "these crusaders are really serious." Slowly the implication of the crusade concept and how it fits into our responsibility to be obedient to God's Word, began to sink in.

Quito, considered one of the most beautiful cities in the western hemisphere, shimmered in the bright afternoon sun. Our flight had been uneventful, and now, more than a mile above sea level, I reveled in my new surroundings. Nestled in the Andes, Quito lies within a few miles of the equator and directly beneath the sparkling snow-cone of Mount Pichincha. The sky is a radiant blue with a depth to it that seems to go on forever. I loved it at first sight.

OMS missionaries picked us up at the airport and gave us a quick tour of the city. Later we had meetings in which they told about the local traditions, offered cultural tips, and prepared us for what was ahead in the next two weeks. We also participated in a lot of prayer--more than I had ever been involved in--and many crusaders gave their testimonies. I was seeing a side of life that was new and exciting. Getting into the spirit of things, I guess I acted like a kid with a new toy. As I look back, those were some of the happiest days of my life.

One of our first adventures was in a poor farming village of about 5,000 people not far from Quito. We were there to pass out tracts and do some door-to-door evangelism, but as we proceeded many of the villagers followed. Capitalizing on our good fortune, we gathered everyone into a group and began to sing, give our testimonies, and hold a service right there on the street. "Boy," I thought, "this sure isn't like Waco."

Several of us were invited into a home, and we talked to those gathered (through our interpreter) about a variety of things, including the fact that there was no church in the village. They explained that the government had built most of the village but made no provision for a church. Families had to pay $6,000 for their apartments, so they had nothing left to spend on a place of worship. I soon discovered that many apartments were for sale; if we could just come up with $6,000 we could furnish them with a church.

Back in Quito that evening I gave this idea a lot of thought, and then went to prayer about it. "Lord," I said, "is this the reason you brought me to Ecuador?" For many days after my prayer I tried to remain sensitive to His guidance, but nothing happened. The week rushed on; we were involved with prayer services, meeting new people, sharing, and handing out tracts. "Lord," I said again, "is this why you brought me to Ecuador?" Again, nothing happened.

Leaving the relative sophistication of the Quito area, we drove over primitive mountain roads in rusty, well-used vehicles--headed for Saraguro where we were to spend our final week. Saraguro is not like Waco either, I can assure you of that. A small village of Ecuadorian Indians, it lies on a mountain range that spawns numbness of mind and body from the constant presence of bone-chilling fog. Under-dressed, brown-skinned children with runny noses stood mesmerized as we unloaded our fancy, store-bought luggage in front of the OMS clinic.

Dr. & Mrs. William Douce have operated the OMS clinic in this remote region for over thirty years. Providing the only medical attention for miles around, they have encoun-tered a tremendous variety of human situations--some tragic, some uplifting. But through their trust in the Lord each and every day, thousands have benefited from their loving skills and spiritual impact.

I remember Dr. Douce vividly. He was continually going at a trot, never slowing his remarkable pace. At that time he was teaching courses on evangelical Christianity at the OMS Bible school in nearby Carboncillo during the week and running the clinic on weekends. I watched as he treated hundreds of patients--even finding time to pray with them. On Saturday night, when you would have expected him to relax for an hour or so in an easy chair, Dr. Douce was preaching in an Indian church located in the village. Then on Sunday morning he preached at a church adjacent to the clinic. He is a robust man of exceptional energy, with every ounce of his vitality focused on the Lord's work.

On Sunday evening we were singing and sharing testimonies in the Douces' conservative apartment adjacent to the clinic, when Ilene Douce began telling us about her daughter. Janet was born in Ecuador but received much of her education in the United States. Now she was about to graduate with a degree in nursing. Nurses were very scarce in this area, therefore very valuable. Enticing a nurse to Saraguro, however, would be analogous to luring a polar bear to Saraguro--something next to impossible. But Janet wanted to come back. In fact, she had already applied to OMS to become a missionary and work with her parents at the Saraguro clinic. How wonderful that must have made Bill and Ilene feel. But first, there was a significant problem to overcome.

As Ilene told of her daughter's desire to return and work with the Indians, tears welled up in her eyes. Hesitating, she said, "It may not happen because Janet needs $6,000 in support before OMS will authorize the assignment." When she expressed how much Bill could use her at the clinic and how badly the Indians needed medical treatment and advice, the tears spilled over onto her cheeks.

"We know that the Lord can provide," she continued, "but Janet is so young and her only contacts are financially strapped college students." Ilene and Bill had been in Ecuador for 32 years and time had taken its toll on the number of their supporters, so Janet couldn't count on help from that source either. But even in this bleak set of circumstances, Ilene ended by simply saying, "We know God is sovereign and has a plan for us. We want nothing more for ourselves than what He wants."

At that moment, while sitting there listening to Ilene, I felt something that's very hard to describe. It was a calming presence of some sort, and all of a sudden my heart, which had been perplexed as to why I was in Ecuador, was comforted. I had never felt such a presence, and it dominated my mind and my will. Even while we traveled back to our room, it stayed with me, in me.

I shared my feelings with Sybil, and we talked about it for a long time. This presence seemed to engulf my soul, and in the quiet of that cool Ecuadorian night I felt humbled--completely unpresuming and free from pride.   Dropping to my knees, I asked Jesus to forgive my sins and to live His life in me from that day forth.   Sybil joined me in prayer, and the Spirit led us to ask if it was because of Janet that we were in Ecuador.   Yes!   The answer wasn't audible, but we had undeniable spiritual assurance that we were there to help Janet--there was no room for doubt.

Rising, we looked at each other in sheer amazement. We both knew we were to help the Douces, and ultimately the Ecuadorians, by adding to the capability of the clinic.   I finally said, "You know, we don't have $6,000.   We would have to sell our home."   Sybil responded in few words but with great authority, "So what?"

Wow!   What a wife.   My head was spinning; so much had happened in such a short time.   Within a matter of an hour or two, in an unfamiliar land and with strangers, I had committed my life to Christ and decided to sell our home. What an uplifting experience.   I didn't feel disturbed or anxious.   In fact, I felt better than I had in years.   I had been appointed to cause an event to happen for Christ--me, not someone you read about in a book.   I was determined to get the job done.

Leaving Ecuador I was filled with abounding joy.   But as the plane headed north, carrying me away from the environment in which I had encountered Christ, I began to wonder how I would achieve my goal.   For hours I wrestled with the issue of raising $6,000, but only one solution surfaced--the selling of our home. "If that's what it takes," I decided, "then that's what we were going to do."

When we arrived in Waco, Sybil and I began to develop a workable plan for selling the house and finding a new place to live. While making a few preliminary contacts, I had the unusual desire to drive down to our church. It was a weekday afternoon and I had no earthly reason to go, yet something urged me to press forward--impelled me, in fact, to go with great haste. I yielded to this thought, and as I pulled into the church parking lot our pastor, Dick Freeman, was getting out of his car. "How was your crusade?" he shouted.

As we approached each other a strange idea crossed my mind. I'm not a person who acts impetuously. In fact, I'm normally on the opposite end of that spectrum. But on this day I wasn't operating normally. When our distance diminished I said, "Dick, I want to talk to you; I would like to have five minutes in the pulpit at each of our three services next Sunday. I realize you've been out of town for a couple of weeks yourself, and I know you're scrambling to get organized right now. But I really need that time. To make matters worse, I can't even tell you exactly how I'm going to use it."

Upon hearing this outlandish request, Dick had a peculiar and quizzical look on his face (who could blame him). In an accommodating, yet pragmatic way, he tried to take control by suggesting I take a full Sunday night service next month. Still not certain why I was making this irregular request, I stuck to my guns. "Dick, we've known each other for a long time. Please, just trust me and give me those five-minute slots. I promise I won't take one minute more."

As Dick slung his coat over his shoulder and we headed into the church, I outlined my plan at about the same speed it was being born in my mind. I told him of my experience in Ecuador, and that I sensed a divine directive to raise $6,000 for Janet Douce to join her parents in their extraordinary ministry at the OMS clinic in Saraguro.

Dick knew I had no experience in the art of presenting a need and could not even qualify as a mediocre speaker. But while we were walking, there was a brief second when we caught each other's eye. Shortly after that, without additional words, Dick agreed to let me have the time.

I went home in mid-air and blurted the news to Sybil, who stood there in utter amazement. She couldn't believe that I had asked to speak at church on Sunday morning. The guy who wouldn't get up in front of the kids at our grandson's birthday party now wanted to address a thousand people. "But the Lord is leading me," I said; and Sybil, in her uncommon ability to penetrate my heart and mind, understood.

There were only two days left, and I spent a lot of that time in prayer. "Lord, speak to me. Whatever you want me to say, I will say. Just give me the message."

Crowding out the darkness of our bedroom, Sunday morning dawned with a brilliant sunrise. Kneeling for one final prayer, I thanked God for the Holy Spirit and for leading me to a saving relationship with Jesus Christ. I thanked Him for Sybil, our church, and our children. But most of all I thanked Him for breaking my heart for those Ecuadorian Indians. I humbly asked for His continued leading and praised Him for the opportunity to serve Him in this way.

I really don't remember rising from the congregation and making my way to the pulpit, but I do know I wasn't nervous. That in itself was some sort of a miracle. I was strong because I knew I had a purpose and that the Lord would help me. I started my presentation by pointing out that in our pews, next to the songbooks, there were cards upon which everyone could make notes. I asked them to take out a card, write the name Janet Douce on it, and place the card in their pocket. Then, in the remaining minutes I explained the situation, asked them to pray about it, and then give any amount they could. I did this for all three services. Each time I could feel the Holy Spirit covering me, filling me with confidence, and directing my words.

The next morning I went to the church office and celebrated with the staff. In one fantastic day we had raised $3,000, half of the entire amount. "This is an example of how the Lord can use individuals," I thought, "and I'm so very glad that He is using *me*."

Next I placed a call to OMS in Greenwood to determine how much money they already had credited to Janet's support. "A good deal came in just recently," they said. "Let's see--it totals $2,500."

Incredible!   We now only needed $500 to meet the goal. In my excitement, and knowing Sybil would approve,   I decided to cover the shortfall. "Praise the Lord!" I said. "Get her ready to go to Ecuador; you'll have a letter of commitment for $3,500 in the mail today and a check just as soon as the money clears our accounting office."   The church office staff was elated--dancing and prancing around. They felt they were joint owners in this worthy and gratifying success.

It wasn't long before Janet called to thank us for raising her support. "I'm packed and on my way to Ecuador," she said, "but I'd like to stop in Waco and personally thank you and your church for underwriting me."   She did, and it was a meeting that excited our congregation.   Hundreds of folks began to experience, firsthand, how they could personally help in the Lord's work.   Instead of just money dropped into a bottomless offering plate, their contributions had life--a mortal in the form of a wonderful, articulate nurse on her way to help an impoverished people.   Sybil and I also received a blessing.   God didn't want us to sell our home after all.   I think He just wanted the commitment.   Instead, we opened our house to traveling missionaries and have been recipients of many additional rewards as a result.

This incident catapulted missions to the forefront of our hearts, and within weeks our church caught the vision. Our first commitment was for Sybil's brother and his family. "Let's take out shares in Mike and Bonnie," she said, "say $50 a month."

"But that's more than we can afford--we're just getting by as it is," I replied.

"You said yourself that when you got up in front of all those people at church you just trusted the Lord," Sybil quipped, "so why not trust Him for this?"

Why not indeed. We signed an OMS faith promise for that amount, and I went to prayer. It wasn't long after--I think we were having lunch together--when the answer came to me. "I've got our $50," I announced; "I know just how we can do it."

By this time Sybil was becoming accustomed to my somewhat unusual behavior. "Surprise me," she said.

I reminded her that we had a $50 monthly membership in a community association, and I saw no reason that it couldn't be eliminated. We could then transfer the money to shares in Mike and Bonnie. We did, and it felt great.

One day at church, a few months later, Pastor Freeman asked me to become chairman of the church missions board. At that time, our church was probably giving $20 a month to OMS mission work. I was thrilled and my spirits soared. What an opportunity to make something happen.

One of my first calls was to Dr. Jim Truitt. Jim and I had just started an MFM council in our church, and he could help me develop an effective mission strategy. "We need some sort of program that will allow us to get more men to the mission field. Once we do that, the Holy Spirit will take over and break their hearts for the lost, just as yours was," he said.

Quickly volunteering, I burst out with, "I can cook! How about having noon luncheons at the church on Sundays? We can raise money to send MFM council members on crusades and even do a whole lot more."

"Let's have at it," said Jim.

Well, we did have at it, starting with a "Sweetheart Lunch" on Valentine's Day. I was the head chef, and I'm pleased to say the program was an immediate success. We turned a handsome profit, and that was just the start.

As the author of this chapter, I titled it *Look What Jesus Did*. Now you will see why.   There's an old adage I remember hearing when I was just a boy. It says, "From small acorns giant oak trees grow." Just as God causes those magnificent trees to grow from tiny seeds, He also caused His work to multiply from the small beginnings I have written about. As a direct result of our crusade to Ecuador, the Holy Spirit has moved across the face of our congregation with such conviction that our mission budget has grown from $20 to $4,900 a month. We now support 47 missionaries and contribute regularly to evangelistic outreaches such as the

OMS Encounter with God program. Some church families, fired by the Holy Spirit, have paid personally for the construction of four churches in India. Dick Freeman, our pastor, went to India to dedicate a seminary named after him and built from mission funds. We have a missions week each year and a strong, effective Men For Missions Council.

Sometimes I just sit back and think about that acorn and what can happen when it is planted and nourished by God's life-giving rains. In I Corinthians 3:6 the great Apostle Paul describes what takes place when men cooperate with God. Paul says, "I planted the seed, Apollos watered it, but God made it grow. So neither he who plants nor he who waters is anything, but only God, who makes things grow" (NIV). I praise God that He directed me, as He did Paul, to plant the seed. I praise Him for allowing hundreds of Christians in our church to water it. But most of all, I humbly thank Him for the increase He provided--for he who plants and he who waters are nothing, it is only by the power of God that such things grow.

You, too, can plant a seed, and as it receives nourishment watch it grow from a tender shoot to a stately tree-- then rejoice with the angels of heaven in the harvest. All you need to do is believe in your heart and say to God:

> I will do whatever You ask me to do;
> I will go wherever You ask me to go;
> I will give whatever You ask me to give.

8

Dale Larrance

*H*ave you ever felt out of place at a meeting? If so, I'm certain Dale Larrance wasn't there. Dale, born and reared in central Illinois, has the magical ability to make the most timid person feel at home. Dale is an MFM cabinet officer, and through his lighthearted spirit our complex and lengthy meetings have become a joy to attend.

Dale is a special prayer warrior, too. Knowing that I travel worldwide, often alone, he prays to guard me against accident and delay. This gives me an added measure of confidence as I ride busses, trains, and taxis in a variety of Third World countries.

Interwoven throughout his jovial personality and deep prayer life is a heartfelt compassion for those not knowing Christ as Savior. Dale is dedicated to Christ's command to reach out and tell others of His saving grace. He has given personal obedience to this edict by traveling to many countries. Working and witnessing for Christ, Dale is another of God's men.

3,800 and Counting

by Dale Larrance

Born in 1923, I was just a child when the Great Depression settled over the land. However, I remember well the hardship it made for our family in rural Illinois. My parents were farmers, and that was one of the occupations hit hardest. In spite of working long hours and careful expenditures, they could provide only the bare necessities.

At age 14 I took a job washing dishes, mopping floors, and doing odd jobs in a restaurant. I don't know how much effect my meager pay had on our family's survivability, but I began to learn the economic lessons of life.

I was glad when I became old enough to enlist in the service. Just graduated from high school, I looked forward to the adventure stretching before me. The Depression was over but money still tight, so I also thought of the steady pay. The fact that there was a war going on was only a minor consideration.

I enlisted in the Marines, and two months later my only brother signed up. Although exposed to combat I was not seriously injured. I wish I could say the same for my brother. He lost his life fighting the Japanese on Saipan in 1944, just one year before the war ended. After all these years, I still miss him a lot.

During a 30-day furlough I gave my high school sweetheart, Betty, an engagement ring. Boy, this was a happy time for us! We made wonderful, exciting plans, and for the first time in my life the future looked bright. At this point I didn't consider that God may have had a hand in selecting Betty to be my wife. Later, as life's complications unfolded, I would be most grateful for her and the spiritual fortitude she provided.

Three weeks after my discharge we were married. To support my bride I worked as a farmhand. Then came the news. Betty was to have our first baby. We rejoiced over our good fortune and prepared for that exciting day. Life was great!

Two weeks before Betty was to deliver, however, the doctor gave a disquieting prognosis; the baby might not be normal. We lived with the unknown for 14 long days. It was a problem I didn't know how to handle. Life, it seemed, had turned on me, and was now my enemy.

Bobby was born with hydrocephalus. His enlarged skull required caesarean procedures. It was a sad day. Here I was--young, strong, healthy, and married to a girl I deeply loved, but with a son who would always be an invalid. It seemed so unfair.

I wallowed in self-pity for quite a while. By my standards Betty should have done the same thing. She not only suffered emotional torment, but the physical pain as well. For the first time I recognized something different about Betty. She coped with this problem better than I did. After all, I was the man of the family and had even been in a war. How could my wife be stronger than I?

That strength was quite evident when she said, "Dale, we'll do what we have to do and accept the responsibility God has given us."

Never once did I hear a bitter word from her. Not until some years later did I realize that her actions were the manifestation of her faith in God.

As the years went by, we were blessed with two healthy daughters and we now have four wonderful grandchildren.

After working as a farmhand for 12 years, I felt my management skills were good enough to operate my own farm. So Betty and I set out on our own. Our frugality and hard work brought a reasonable degree of success, but success didn't bring the things I thought it would. In fact, I became more and more restless.

It began to dawn on me that Betty had an inner peace that I lacked. Bobby required total care, and the other children needed their mother as well. When I considered the demands I put on her, I wondered how she withstood the stress. She even had time for church.

As time went on I began assigning more importance to her faith. I went to church, too, but did a lot of day-dreaming during the sermon. When the service was over I left its meaning in the pew. I was free for another week. But then I began to recognize the practical side of Betty's convictions. It was the foundation upon which her fortitude and perseverance were built.

I mentally acknowledged her spirituality and in my simple way decided I should do something to prove my worth, too. I zeroed in on smoking. Betty had been trying to get me to quit for years, and even prayed for me. But now, for the first time, I took the smoking issue seriously. In fact, I even prayed about it--a totally new adventure for me.

I was 45 years old and smoked two packs of cigarettes a day, but I still managed to quit. I'm certain, however, it was because of Betty's prayers, not mine, as I had yet to give the Lord my heart.

Knowing Betty's position with Christ was far more secure than mine weighed heavy on my heart. About a year later I sat at our kitchen table drinking coffee with our pastor. He sensed my restlessness and began to read from the Bible.

"For it is with your heart that you believe and are justified, and it is with your mouth that you confess and are saved" (Romans 10:10 NIV).

As he counseled me, I felt closer to the Lord than at any time in my life. His voice cracked with emotion as he resumed reading: "For everyone who calls on the name of the Lord will be saved" (Romans 10:13 NIV).

Under deep conviction, I confessed my sins and invited Christ into my life--the best decision of my life.

I learned later that my single act of obedience was the culmination of 25 years of Betty's prayers. I was now a Christian--but I didn't know how to live like one.

For the next three years I went to church and listened to the sermons intently. But I sat in the back and really didn't believe anything else was required. Now I understand how Satan can blind us. When I consider how I allowed him to limit my effectiveness for Christ, I boil with anger.

In the course of time I attended a Men For Missions banquet sponsored by our church. Max Edwards, the speaker, interested me because he had been a farmer, like me. Even though he was a missionary in Brazil, I knew I could identify with another man of the soil.

We had the usual motel meal--starchy potatoes, greasy chicken, and cold peas--but Max made it all worthwhile. He began by showing slides of work OMS has accomplished in Brazil. Then he told about a chapel he wanted to build at the youth camp where he worked. He was forming a crusade of Christian laymen to go down and build it. He needed two more men.

At that moment I heard the voice of the Holy Spirit. I was to go. Me, a dirt farmer from central Illinois, going all the way to South America to build a chapel for Christ. What a change of events. I couldn't wait to tell Betty.

But Betty already knew something big was brewing. The Holy Spirit had influenced her as well. She was thoroughly delighted. I found no difficulty in meeting the second part of MFM's three-point pledge--to go wherever God asks me to go.

Although the crusade was to leave in two weeks, I managed to obtain a birth certificate. I could never have opened those bureaucratic doors that quickly without God's help.

There were twenty men on this crusade. It was hot and the work hard, but I was so excited about being a part of God's cause I hardly noticed the discomfort. I carried block, mixed cement, and learned the skills of a brick mason "overnight".

As our team worked together a bond of fellowship developed. We exchanged testimonies. I told them how Bobby's birth affected me and how Betty's response was part of God's plan to bring me to salvation. They related their experiences and I saw God's sovereignty in their lives, too.

We had devotions every morning, shared our faith during the day, and prayed together in the evening. We were no longer individuals but a unified instrument of God, sharply focused on a single objective--saving souls.

The walls of the chapel rose daily. Two feet--four feet; then obscure openings became functional windows and doors. Finally the walls were completed, an event which arrived simultaneously with the end of the crusade. The roof would have to wait.

We gathered in the chapel. As I sat there, the moon and stars never seemed more beautiful. In song and prayer we worshiped God from the depths of our hearts. Then I heard a petition I will never forget:

"O God, we have toiled to build this chapel so others might come to worship You. We have love in our hearts, and our hands have worked with the strength You provide. Each brick has been placed to honor You and bring salvation to the lost.

"Lord, we pray that for each brick laid, one soul will be saved. The walls contain 3,800 bricks. We ask that the fruit of our labor bring 3,800 lost souls to heaven's gates."

My last night in Brazil was bitter-sweet. I was not ready to leave. I had discovered new relationships with other Christians, and more importantly, with God--a bonding I had never before experienced.

I returned to Illinois and Betty a changed man.

Now I realized that God could use *me*, a simple farmer. I also learned He could use me at home. In fact, there was much to do. I accepted a responsible office in our church, prayed regularly for missionaries, gave missionaries financial support, and joined the local Men For Missions council.

God gave me a burning, intense desire to give personal obedience to the Great Commission: "Go into all the world and preach the good news to all creation" (Mark 16:15 NIV).

Not only did I have the desire, but Romans 10:14-15 challenged me with the practical reasons to do so: "How then can they call on the one they have not believed in? And how can they believe in the one of whom they have not heard? And how can they hear without someone preaching to them? And how can they preach unless they are sent? As it is written, 'How beautiful are the feet of those who bring good news!'"

God has allowed me to satisfy my new desire by sharing the good news on 19 Men For Missions crusades. Most of my work for Christ--building, witnessing, and praying--has been in Brazil, but I've also served in Colombia, Ecuador, and Spain. My life has been greatly enriched by the experiences in each of these countries.

I was also blessed by another unusual opportunity. Traveling thousands of miles, I accompanied MFM's Eastern Regional Director, Max Edwards*. Max covered all the U.S east of the Mississippi, and as we visited MFM councils, I fellowshiped with hundreds of God's children. Words cannot express how precious that time was for me.

On one of these excursions I saw a new video on Brazil. It spoke of missionaries and exciting new programs and projects. Then, as I watched, God touched my heart in a most unexpected way. A missionary told how MFMers built a chapel ten years ago. He mentioned the long hours, hard work, and the heat. He also told about our prayer--a soul to be saved for each of the chapel's 3,800 bricks. Then, smiling broadly, he announced:

"Records now indicate that over 3,800 men, women, and young adults have found Christ within the chapel's walls."

Tears furrowed my cheeks as God put a love in my heart which will last forever.

I am so unworthy to be part of such a great movement. I can only thank Betty for her spiritual guidance, Men For Missions for the opportunity to serve, and Jesus Christ for His love and forgiving grace. I intend to serve Him faithfully each day of my life.

---

*Max Edwards is now the OMS Field Director for Mexico.

9

Stan Ross

*W*ith the mention of my friend Stan Ross, several positive attributes immediately come to my mind. He is hospitable, generous, and a capable communicator. He's also a man with firm belief in Jesus Christ and deep understanding of the need for a Savior.

Most of us living north of the Mason-Dixon line speak warmly of those in the southern states as being hospitable and gracious. One of my delights has been the discovery of those same characteristics in the people of Ireland, Stan's home. Unfortunately we often generalize with aphorisms like "the luck of the Irish" or "the fighting Irish." But my personal impressions lead me to label them "the congenial and generous Irish."

I'm certain that you will draw positive insights from this Irishman's testimony. Among other things the tenacity with which he clings to his Savior, Jesus Christ. Now a Canadian citizen, Stan loves a good story and possesses a great sense of humor. Yet as you look deeply into the man's soul you find a person of great spiritual wealth and commitment--a man you love to be with as he sharpens your life.

Those Incredible Seeds

by Stan Ross

Unlike many young men in Ireland, I was brought up in a staunch Christian home where itinerant missionaries and evangelists commonly stayed overnight. These men of God even bounced me on their knees when I was just a baby. Having spent my formative years in a Christian atmosphere, I was well grounded in Christianity. But I wasn't saved until the age of 18, and only after life had handed me a number of turbulent and unnerving experiences.

I lived in the small, coastal town of Donaghadee in the north of Ireland. On summer evenings young men would gather at the old lighthouse nearby and sing hymns--especially those relating to the sea. As a young lad I would go there and listen to favorites such as "Let the Lower Lights be Burning" and "Farther Along". One that particularly impressed me was "See the Waves and Billows Roll". Little did I suspect that the words of that song would play a part in my conversion, or that one of the lighthouse singers would unexpectedly reappear in my life decades later.

Then came those terrible war years. I joined the Red Cross and at age 16 was shipped to London as an ambulance driver. I drove behind fire trucks threading their way down narrow streets partially blocked by fallen trees and buildings--many still burning. The roaring onslaught of bombers, the wail of air-raid sirens, pencil-thin searchlights, and the thunder-roll of bombs falling in the distance created great anxiety in my heart. I can still recall the emptiness I felt while making my way through the rubble, picking up the dead and dying as red-orange flames danced about. Screams and pleas for help were commonplace, as sortie after sortie of Hitler's Luftwaffe dropped their deadly fireballs.

Through those horrifying experiences I realized that my own death was a real possibility. Where would I spend eternity? I was very glad when I finally earned a leave and was allowed to go home for a few weeks. Even though my leave was for a short period, I decided to attend daily revivals held by an evangelist known for his "fire and brimstone" preaching. With the anguish of war burning in my mind, I heard him state that one day you can be alive and well and the next day dead--with grass growing green on your grave in only six months. "Where would your soul be?" he asked pointedly. I agonized for days over that question. An impending disaster seemed to hang over me like the sword of Damocles, suspended by a single hair. I was truly disturbed and bewildered. Although I wanted to accept the Lord, it seemed that all my efforts to do so failed. I tried to make myself believe, make myself trust; I read my Bible daily and I prayed. But then I would get up and say, "Lord, I'm not saved yet, what's wrong?"

On the last night of the revival, I walked to the bus stop (about a mile away) with a young friend who had accepted the Lord the previous night. I so wanted what he now possessed. How strange and frustrating, I thought--growing up in a Christian home, completely surrounded by examples of faith and regularly seeing prayers answered, yet not knowing what to do to be saved.

We arrived at a bridge and waited there for the bus. Heavy rain clouds hung low in the sky, and the wind chilled my bones. As I looked into the swollen, brackish water a feeling of desperation swept over me. Then out of the distant past a hymn those young men sang at the lighthouse flooded my mind:

See the waves and billows roll
For His sinless, spotless soul;
Oh, my soul, it was for thee,
Praise Him, praise Him cheerfully.

Suddenly it hit me. *"That's it!"* I exclaimed in a loud voice.

"What's it?" said my friend.

"The Lord came to earth to die on the cross just to save me, and it's already done! All I have to do is believe it."

"Why, of course," he said. "What had you been thinking?"

How simple it all seemed now. In spite of all the instruction I received, all the scripture I memorized, and all the theology I learned--it was the simple, yet heartfelt verse of a hymn that led me to the Lord.

Looking into the night sky I wholeheartedly declared, "Praise be to God Almighty." At that moment my body warmed, and it seemed as though a great oppression lifted from me. My life was changed and I knew it. The anxieties disappeared and I rejoiced in my new-found salvation. With a smile on my face, I arrived home and opened my Bible. The first verse that spoke to me was John 5:24, "He that heareth my Word and believeth...."

"Others must also hear His Word," I whispered, "and I'm going to spend my life telling them." That was in 1943 and the Lord has helped me keep that promise.

A few months later I attended a large revival with friends on the streets of Belfast. Since I was newly saved, they must have thought I was a prime candidate to give a testimony. Pushing me off the crowded sidewalk and into the street, they shouted, "This man's just been converted," and "Tell us all about it."

I didn't know what to say. I was caught completely off guard. Struggling for words, I bought a few seconds of time by reciting lines of an old poem--for some strange reason, the only thing I could think of. I'm sure I appeared silly when I started with, "Laugh and the whole world laughs with you, weep and you weep alone." Nevertheless, that's what I did.

"What a trick to pull on a new Christian," I thought, as the crowd snickered at my inexperience. Then, when I got into my testimony, a young man in the crowd began cursing and interrupting me. What a dilemma. Can you imagine this scene? Picture yourself in the middle of a big-city street, completely surrounded by noisy townspeople, embarrassed in front of friends, and while you are trying to tell an unlikely group how Jesus came into your life someone screams curses at you. My knees were like water, my voice quivered, and my heart was pounding. I know it was only through the power of the Holy Spirit that I managed to get through that testimony. I certainly didn't expect it to bear fruit. In fact, I felt like a failure and was quite disillusioned about the whole ordeal.

Through the healing graces of our Lord, however, I managed to recover from my anguish. In fact, I even received an extra blessing; somehow I seemed to develop more confidence in my position with Christ. Did He not say, "Blessed are you when people insult you, persecute you and falsely say all kinds of evil against you because of me" (Matthew 5:11 NIV).

With my new-found courage displayed like a badge on my chest, I went to another open-air revival in a different Irish town. It was a bleak, rainy day--gusty winds and the cold salt air kept people in their homes, and we were disappointed in the turnout. Standing on a street corner surveying the situation, my friends considered leaving. Then just as we turned to go, I unexpectedly experienced the influence of the Holy Spirit, receiving both energy and a desire to witness.

As we stood next to a small, whitewashed cottage on this wind-swept corner, I followed the Spirit's lead and began to give my testimony. My friends looked at me as though I were out of my mind. I can't blame them; only the four of us were there and they had heard it before. "I know my Redeemer liveth"...I began; then for their benefit I quickly inserted, "Just for practice, fellows," and continued without missing a word.

After the war came to an end my friend, Dave Mc-Kinelin, and I began to evangelize in northern Ireland by handing out tracts and preaching in a rented hall. I was only 21 at the time, but the Holy Spirit had broken my heart for the unsaved and set me aflame to witness and preach. We were staying in the modest home of a 70-year-old lady who had befriended Dave and offered us free lodging. A devout Christian, she believed in us and wanted to help bring Christ to the people of her city. Although we didn't know it, this lovely lady gave up her bed and slept on the kitchen floor for the first two nights we were there. Can you imagine such faithfulness? When we discovered what was happening we put a stop to it, but what a witness that was. Even today her unwavering dedication to Christ continues to kindle the flame in my heart.

This particular area of Ireland was 95% Roman Catholic, but Dave and I got down on our hands and knees to pray that people would come to our service. I was greatly encouraged when a few did attend. On the other hand we stirred up a hornets' nest among the city's residents. They weren't accustomed to outsiders coming into town and trying to "woo people away from the Catholic church." They were so angry they even tried to disrupt our services and chase us out of town. Growing crowds surrounded us, cursing and throwing stones at the hall. On two occasions, we had to have a police escort to leave the building safely.

Some years later, and after much prayer, I moved from Ireland to Canada, hoping to attain a better economic future. I attended the local Methodist church and was subsequently invited to a meeting of the Toronto Council of Men For Missions. I had no idea what MFM was all about, but it sounded interesting so I decided to find out. It soon became evident that they were men after my own heart. They believed in God and His work through missions, and weren't afraid to let it be known. While there I learned of an MFM retreat scheduled for the following month at Miner's Bay, so I signed up. I remember wondering if God had a hand in leading me to this new organization.

When I arrived at Miner's Bay, they were out of private rooms so they put me with a chap named John McHardy. John, I learned, had been the OMS national director in Canada for a number of years, and had a strong association with Men For Missions. I took an immediate liking to him and we became fast friends. One evening, just before retiring for the night, I discovered that John was from Ireland, too. Not only that, he often went to Donaghadee.

"That's where I'm from, John. Do you remember the old lighthouse that used to be there?"

"Sure do," he quipped. "Some of us guys used to go out there on balmy evenings to socialize and sing hymns and songs of the sea."

In utter amazement I pursued my questioning. "John, do you remember one that went,

> *"See the waves and billows roll*
> *For His sinless, spotless soul?"*

He responded with,

> *"Oh my soul it was for thee,*
> *Praise Him, praise Him cheerfully."*

Tears welled up in my eyes as I remembered how those words helped bring me to salvation while standing on an Irish bridge so long ago. John sensed my spiritual emotion, and we embraced. He never dreamed that the hymn he sang 27 years ago would bear such fruit. And now God was letting both of us in on His little secret. Soon thereafter the Lord produced even more fruit from unlikely seeds sown in the past.

I remember attending a church meeting in Toronto not long after that in which a missionary doctor from Africa was speaking. After the meeting I had the privilege of talking to him over a cup of coffee. Like John, he was from Ireland. As our conversation proceeded, we zeroed in on a particular street revival. Would you believe that this man of God was the same chap that hurled insults and curses at me when I tried to give my testimony to that noisy crowd in Belfast 25 years earlier?

The bottom had fallen out of his world at that time, he told me. Deeply depressed, he had turned to alcohol, and on that day was quite inebriated. Even so, my testimony, like a sharp two-edged sword, had penetrated his verbal defenses and drunken condition. He said he went home feeling different--as if he were being uplifted--and in the quiet of his bedroom that night gave his heart to Jesus. He then related how he went to medical school and subsequently felt God's call to Africa--to minister to those with both physical and spiritual needs.

I stood there flabbergasted. A soul saved and a life given to Christ's work from my clumsy attempt to give my witness? "Only by the power of God," I thought. Silently I prayed, "Father, thank You for using me and allowing me to know of this miracle."

Three years later I was speaking in another meeting in Toronto when a lady with graying hair caught my attention. Motioning me to the side she said, "I'm glad to hear you're from Ireland--that's my home too, and I want to ask you something. Are you the same man who stood on the corner of Manor Street and gave a testimony?"

My mind darted back to that rainy day many years ago when I gave my testimony "just for practice."

"Aren't you the one who started your testimony with, "I know my Redeemer liveth...?"

"Why--uh--yes," I responded, again not knowing what to say.

"Well, I just want you to know I was sitting behind the curtains in that white cottage and heard every word you said. I thought you were speaking to those other chaps and I was eavesdropping. But I was so enthralled by your words I couldn't pull away. I dropped to my knees and gave my heart to Jesus as soon as you finished."

"God does work in mysterious ways, doesn't He?" I stammered. Smiling, she brushed a tear from my cheek. And again I lifted praise to God. How very sweet is the fruit of His vineyard.

"You're a carpenter. Can you go to Haiti to put a roof on the OMS clinic?"

I recognized the voice on the phone as that of Don Peneycad, president of the Toronto MFM council. "They need a man down there to help with this roof problem right away; other crusaders are tied up building a radio tower." Having attended several MFM council meetings, I had been exposed to the crusade program and often wondered what it would be like to go. When I heard Don's voice, it was like getting a call from Jesus. I didn't have any trouble deciding to go.

Being in Haiti was a real breakthrough for me. Having missionaries in and out of our home during my formative years made them an interesting and exciting group of people, and I often wondered what a mission field was like. I had read missionary books--even one by David Livingstone--and had given money to missions for years. I felt this was designed by the Lord to "round me out."

I worked in the sweltering heat right alongside the nationals; sweating was easy as we put the roof on the dental clinic, hung doors, and installed windows. But the fellowship I experienced with the nationals and the missionaries made it worthwhile. Although I was doing what I was familiar with, carpentry work, the crusade was a tremendous learning experience. Even though tired, we had stimulating conversations with the OMS Bible school students in the evenings. We went to different churches with them, walked through fields of sugar cane, and sat on cool benches as we swapped stories of Christ's blessings. I even had time to be a matchmaker.

A nurse there, Faith Jones, lived with two other nurses. Dave Clark, a bachelor crusader, and I were scheduled to have lunch at their house. Faith was supposed to keep us entertained while the other two prepared the meal. The conversation was lagging, however, and Dave was twiddling his thumbs. So I started to joke around a bit, just to take the edge off.

"Faith," I said, "is it because Dave is here that you don't take your turn in the kitchen? You two would make a good pair."

They both blushed, their eyes dropped, and my comments did nothing to stimulate the conversation. But they must not have gone unnoticed because a year later Dave and Faith were married. I still remember the day I received the news. "It's happened again!" I thought. "How little we know the impact our words have on the lives of others."

A few years passed and I decided it was time to go again. So I signed up for an MFM witness crusade to Ecuador. I suppose I had the most pleasurable time of my life on this crusade--and I owe it all to a champion Christian named George Carnett. I learned a lot on this crusade, too. Not only did I see mission work in Quito, Guayaquil, and Carboncillo, I saw a level of spiritual darkness that has made me sensitive to Ecuador's needs ever since.

I want to tell you about George, but I'll begin by describing a crusade misfit named Kevin (a fictitious name). Somehow this fellow slipped through the MFM crusade application process and was not spiritually prepared for the experience. He was easy to identify by his long hair, green Fighting Irish T-shirt (which he wore for six days), and the constant use of a Sony "Walkman" radio. George, on the other hand, was on the opposite end of the spectrum. He was interested in only one thing--bringing sinners to Christ.

Perhaps I can best explain the difference between these two men by example. While still at the airport in Miami, Kevin bragged about the high salary he received as a railroad engineer in one breath and in the next told how members of a group of youngsters he was discipling paid for his trip to Ecuador. When I heard these seemingly contradictory circumstances, I turned to George (who was a stranger at this time) and said, "It must be nice to earn all that money and have someone else pay for your trip." George responded by opening his Bible and preaching to me about the virtue of not judging one another.

When we arrived in Quito, guess who my roommates were. Yes, Kevin and George. I was beginning to wish I had never come, but as it worked out Kevin was a catalyst that drew George and me close together. The first thing Kevin did was to tell me, without prompting, I might add, that he hated me because I was a father image and he hated his father. He then went out in the hallway and began to smoke a cigarette. Well, George and I got down on our knees and began praying for his smoking habit and his broken relationship with his father (MFM believes in a separated lifestyle and does not want to tarnish Christ's image on the mission field by sending crusaders who smoke or drink).

George must have decided that I was all right after all, because after I gave devotions on the second day, he flopped down next to me on the bus and said, "Would you mind if I sit beside you? You're the kind of guy I can relate to." From that point on, George stuck to me like glue, and nothing could have made me happier.

By the evening of that day we discovered that Kevin didn't know how to pray. His idea of praying was to repeat the same words over and over, "Praise the Lord, Praise His Name, Praise the Lord." George took it on himself to give Kevin instructions, and I backed him up by citing scripture.

We did this every night before we went to bed, and I awoke each morning to find George on his hands and knees praying for this fellow.

We're not sure to this day what happened to Kevin. He must have decided he was with the wrong group, because about halfway through the crusade he packed his bags and left for home. I still pray for Kevin--I know how God works, and I know the power of a good witness. Kevin was exposed to that witness, and the Hound of heaven will be faithful no matter where he is today.

A week later the crusade was over and we headed home, as well. After boarding our return flight in Quito, George found a seat next to a middle-aged Ecuadorian. With Christ's love built into his character, George couldn't resist a chance to witness. So once we were airborne he put his hand on the man's shoulder and said, "Friend, Jesus loves you."

The Ecuadorian recoiled from his touch, looked at him in disgust, and said, "Get lost!"

I couldn't help overhearing, and I whispered, "Take it easy, George; you can't approach people that abruptly--slow down, and ease into it." He grunted a confirmation, but a few minutes later I noticed George was writing a note. Not just a line or two, it was a full page. He folded it and, to my dismay, handed it to the man.

Instinctively I said, "George, leave the man alone." But it was too late. The man looked at the note for about ten seconds, then with narrowed eyes, slowly and deliberately tore the note into pieces and threw them on the floor.

At first George was wide-eyed, then he sank into a state of visible disappointment. In an effort to comfort him I explained that each morning I ask the Lord to guide me through the day, and if He wants me to witness to anyone, to bring him across my path. I used an example of someone asking me about my (MFM) lapel pin, thereby opening a conversation and allowing me to witness. "I never openly confront someone with the gospel, George, I wait until they come to me. I've seen this approach work hundreds of times." George concurred, although somewhat reluctantly.

Due to our flight schedules we had to stay overnight in Miami. It was late and both of us were famished, so we checked into a hotel and headed for the dining room. After eating, George and I were the last ones to leave. At the door we passed a large, smelly man that reminded me of kaleidoscope images I saw as a child. Leaning against the door frame, he was wearing a bright red jacket, a black and white striped shirt, white pants, suspenders, and black and white wing-tips. A bald head and a cigar protruding from a fat, ruddy face topped off his appearance.

His demeanor matched his dress. From behind a cloud of blue-gray smoke, the man clamped his hand on George's arm and blurted, "What's exciting in your life, guy?"

George, without missing a beat, responded, "Jesus is exciting in my life. Did you ever meet the Lord Jesus?" He started witnessing to this man at once. I was a few paces ahead of George so just walked on and returned to our room. About thirty minutes later George burst through the door. He was absolutely ecstatic--smiling, dancing around, and yelling, "It works! It works! I'm going to get a bigger MFM lapel pin!"

Crusades are a wonderful way to experience other cultures and see firsthand how Christ is working. Along the way you may even meet colorful characters like George did. I was in Toronto a few weeks ago speaking about crusades and how Christians in other lands can be persecuted for their beliefs. For an example I told of the time in Ireland when Dave McKinelin and I held services in the rented hall, and the young men of the town threw stones at the building.

At the conclusion of my sermon a man approached me with, "You're not going to believe this, but I was one of the guys who threw those stones at you 42 years ago." He introduced himself as Bill Bell and told how he and a buddy had participated in the attacks. He went on to say that his friend succumbed to the preaching he heard coming from inside the hall and gave his life to Christ at the hall door. Bill, seeing this happen, began placing value on the words emanating from our services and he, too, was saved outside the building.

Although surprised by this news, I wasn't as shocked as in earlier encounters with my past. Over the years the Lord has shown me many times that the words we speak have immeasurable value. The lesson is simple. If your words are in Christ's will, they have immense power--a potency you may not even suspect exists, but that's not a confirmation that it doesn't. The book of Hebrews tells us: "For the Word of God is living and active. Sharper than any double-edged sword, it penetrates even to dividing soul and spirit, joints and marrow; it judges the thoughts and attitudes of the heart" (Hebrews 4:12 NIV).

Your witness allows others to see what Jesus has done for you and what He means to you--it gives them a human reference to focus on. You can give your witness on television or have big campaigns, but I've found that a personal witness--speaking one to one and eye to eye--bears the sweetest fruit. Men For Missions provides an excellent opportunity for such testimony. People see MFMers as leading lives of honesty and purity. They admire that and want the same for themselves. You might even say that's the purpose of MFM. How exciting it is to see our witness multiplied in the most unexpected and astonishing ways.

10

Ron Mertens

*R*on Mertens is not a difficult man to get to know. He is quiet--perhaps intense would be a better word--and knows where he's going. Since a life-changing accident three years ago, and subsequent commissioning as an OMS missionary, he has become a highly valued Men For Missions resource. I owe a tremendous debt to him, not only for bringing the *Action* magazine back into circulation, but also for his help in writing this book.

Though MFM looks for men who have been tested by the fires of life, few have experienced anything like the test

Ron has undergone. Through the mercies of Christ he passed with flying colors and continues to recognize the Lord's hand working in his life.

I am reminded of the trials of Joseph, how Satan meant them for evil, but God turned them into good. Many prayed that Ron's experience in Colombia would bring glory to Christ. Those prayers were marvelously answered.

The Potter and the Clay

by Ron Mertens

It took a long time before I responded to God's call. Not that He didn't keep calling. I just wasn't listening. Equipped with an over-supply of drive, youth, and physical strength, I had my *own* agenda. Who needed God?

But let me start at the beginning. When I was a youngster I went to church and Sunday school regularly (I remember getting gold stars for perfect attendance). My mother taught me to pray before going to bed, and our family prayed at each meal. At the age of 13 I attended confirmation class, where I learned the mechanics of prayer and scripture memorization. I was then accepted into the church. By this time I had learned responsibility, knew the difference between right and wrong, and was living a decent moral life. I thought I was "OK" and that was enough--not realizing life is never complete without a personal relationship with Jesus.

This one flaw, however, made Satan very happy. After high school, I was really exposed to the world's temptations, and the basic training of my youth began to erode. Little by little, assorted temptations lured me closer and closer to the deceiver's camp. By the time I entered the Indiana State Police Recruit School at age 21, my standards consisted of an attempt to be honest and a "nice guy". Admirable, no doubt, but standards of the world.

For the next 29 years I worked as a state police officer. When I recall those years I must pause and give thanks to the Lord for being so patient with me, so gracious, so long-suffering. I certainly had no time for Him. I was preoccupied with steering wheels and gunpowder.

But God was not only patient, He also gave His divine protection. As a trooper my beat was Interstate 65, which enters Indiana just north of Louisville, Kentucky. In those days the speed limit on the interstate was 70 mph, and drivers received warning tickets until they hit 80. I observed drunks and speeders exceeding that limit daily. If they were going the opposite direction, I had to turn around and catch them before I could "clock" them. To accomplish that, I drove at extremely high pursuit speeds, often running flat out at 130 mph--sometimes in bad weather. It was my job to investigate hundreds of traffic accidents--many times extricating screaming people from their bone-shattering collisions. I've walked in their blood on the highway.

As time went on I became well acquainted with all the hate, violence, greed, and tragedy man can bring upon himself. I investigated thefts, burglaries, rapes, and robberies. I've seen blood and brains dripping from ceilings as a result of "shotgun-in-the-mouth" suicides. I've recovered bodies, bloated beyond recognition, from rivers and lakes. I've brushed maggots off murder victims found in the woods and dug bullets out of ground soaked with their blood. I helped pick up the remains of 85 people killed in a mid-air collision, and I've attended the autopsies of over 50 victims killed by other assorted acts of violence.

I tell you this because hostility, destruction, and death--in their grossest forms--were my business. It was just part of my job, and I took it all in stride. Too much so, in fact. I began to see death as representing nothing more than the broken dreams of the unlucky. I gave no thought about what lies beyond the grave. After all, I had "lady-luck" riding right on my hip. Unknown to me, however, it was God that was protecting me for another job--one for which I had to be carefully molded.

The constant exposure to this lifestyle took its toll. I became cynical and restless--hard. I countered internal conflicts by becoming very efficient at my work. Even worse,

I became self-sufficient. I was the captain of my life. I didn't need religion.

I soon began to make recognition from man my god. I became a workaholic--earning a bachelor's and master's degree while working 50 hours a week. I received promotion after promotion, each with more responsibility. This I told myself, was success.

Before long I was made director of the Indiana State Police Crime Laboratory Division, a system of four labs employing 60 specialists. Later I accepted directorship of the agency's Training and Personnel Division. My life became highly technical. It was also a spiritual wasteland. Before I learned that nice guys don't cut it spiritually, I thought this was "it." Then, just before my heart got *too* hard, the Holy Spirit nudged me.

I watched Billy Graham on television a few times when nothing else was on and gained a few insights into God's Word. Memories of my youth began to surface--grandfather saying grace at mealtime, mother by my bed teaching me to pray, and going to church and Sunday school. I began to feel God's leading and became aware of my own personal desert. Now I felt less confident in myself, less self-sufficient. For the first time in my life, I considered eternity.

At that point the Holy Spirit really took my hand. He led me to the Community Church of Greenwood where I answered an altar call. When the invitation was given I made my way down the aisle so fast they didn't know what to do with me. I needed no pleading or persuasion. I didn't have to "get up the nerve". I was eager, it was as though the Holy Spirit put wheels under my feet. I'll never forget the wonderful feeling of peace that resulted from that commitment.

I was baptized a few months later. With Jesus living in my heart, my standards abruptly changed. They were no longer those of the world--just being a nice guy--but the standards of Christ. I finally had found the "right stuff."

Now I wanted to work for Christ, not for myself. I had a heart full of love--a servant's heart--for the first time in my life. The more humble the task the more I sought it--the more I enjoyed doing it. I volunteered many hours at the church--painting, planting shrubs, cutting grass, shoveling gravel--and loved it. God was doing a great work in my life. It was a beautiful experience--like washing feet.

I soon became chairman of the church building and grounds committee, and my wife, Ila, and I led a Bible Fellowship group. But that wasn't enough. Motivated by the Holy Spirit I wanted to do more.

"More" took shape in the form of an MFM work crusade to Medellin, Colombia. A cold January found us trudging through Indiana snows to a variety of medical centers for inoculations. In spite of the "square needles," our enthusiasm prevailed. Ecstatic over the prospect of serving the Lord for two weeks on a mission field, we crossed each day off our calendar. Everything was in perfect order.

Late one Saturday evening our plane landed on an Andean mountaintop near Medellin, the "City of Perpetual Spring." Led by Ron Collins, an experienced MFM staffer, we were cheerfully received by two missionaries from the OMS seminary. Ten of us squeezed into an aged bus, which was already overflowing with luggage and badly needed electrical supplies. It groaned and creaked as we maneuvered down the serpentine highway toward the city. Tired, but full of joy, we watched the mountains gradually give way to foothills as we approached the OMS seminary.

Although it was long past the missionaries' usual bedtime, we were greeted warmly. Someone called us to prayer, and we all gave thanks for our safe arrival and earnestly asked that our work would be effective. Ila and I were billeted with Dave and Carol Cosby, missionaries who not only taught at the seminary but also had grounds and building maintenance responsibilities.

The next morning Dave asked if I would give my testimony at the seminary's Sunday morning service. I'm glad the Lord gave me that opportunity, because it allowed the students to see the person they were soon to hear so much about.

That afternoon crusaders and seminary staff mixed casually over a fried chicken lunch on Cosbys' veranda. We talked about our families, homes, and jobs--then sang heart warming Christian songs. We felt lovingly bonded together with these Colombians and missionaries in the family of Christ.

Later the crusaders went into a huddle to receive work assignments. A tour of the job site gave us our first glimpse of what lay ahead. The roof of an old, but sound, storage building was to be removed so its walls could be raised. Once a new roof was installed, the building would have a functional second floor. Monday would come soon enough, however. That night we sang more songs, ate cold chicken, and enjoyed a majestic view of Medellin as thousands of city lights sparkled in the cool Andean air. Refreshed and invigorated by the love of Christ, Ila and I slept well that night.

The next morning we ate a hearty breakfast and, unable to restrain our excitement, arrived at the work site twenty minutes early. While Ila distributed supplies, I helped remove a wooden loft and then began repairs on a rickety staircase. From that vantage point I could look through the rafters and see several crusaders on the roof removing large sections of slate. A few minutes later I stood on the roof myself, trying not to look down while helping with the slate and enjoying the fantastic view.

Suddenly I began a terrifying journey of discovery--one that crosses the gulf between life and death. I remember an earsplitting roar as the roof collapsed under my feet and blurry objects flashed across my vision. With my arms flailing, my ribs raked across a support beam and a nail ripped my arm. My thoughts broke into fragments.

I was on the way down. Suddenly I hit the concrete floor--hard! Roofing slate and dirt-covered rafters engulfed me. As I came to my senses, a disconcerting silence filled the building. The roar was gone--in its place was an excruciating pain in my back. My agony flared, dominating everything. My eyes were welded shut, my thoughts disjointed, my screaming voice cracked with pain.

For a single terrifying moment, great fear swept over me, controlling me. Without doubt my life would soon be over.

Centered in my lower back, earth-pounding pain soared through my body as the sensation of crushed bone assaulted my nervous system. A raw and penetrating dread of death overwhelmed me. I felt destroyed, with no possible hope of recovery. The pain extended itself at will, erupting into a devastating crescendo that engulfed my body. A different pain now--my left foot. Is it broken, too? Instinctively, as a drowning man reaches for a branch, I cried out, "Jesus, help me! Jesus, *please* help me!"

At that instant I was relieved of my dreadful and diabolical panic. I felt the Holy Spirit's sustaining calm fill my body, totally replacing my terror. The pain remained--terrible as it was--but like wisps of smoke my fear vanished.

All work ceased. The room remained silent. Then action replaced immobility. Two crusaders rushed to my side: Bob McKaig--who had fallen with me but was protected and came through the ordeal unscathed--and Ron Collins, our crusade leader. In the trauma of that moment I heard them pray for me--begging for the Lord's care and mercy.

Time seemed suspended. People became animated figures. Voices ebbed and flowed like surging swells. Ila was devastated. I recognized the voice of Jeannie Wittig, the seminary nurse. She shouted commands--first protecting me then sending a Colombian scurrying for a board.

He arrived instantaneously with a board of perfect dimensions--one which could support me and still navigate the bends through hallways and doors. "How did he manage that?" I wondered. But I soon learned to expect such miracles; my Lord had me under His priceless protection.

I was carefully carried to a waiting jeep, where a doctor awaited me. "Another miracle?" I wondered. Dr. David Brabon, a plastic surgeon with ties to the seminary, had arrived early from Bogota due to a scheduling error. As the jeep pulled away, he began examining me. With Jeannie holding my hand and Ila encouraging me, we bounced down rough cobblestone streets to the hospital.

While Dr. Brabon searched for an orthopedic specialist, I was held in a large lobby. Overhead I could see a limp Colombian flag on a long staff. A pharmacy occupied the center of the foyer. Curious glances from "people who could walk" surveyed me. Still in excruciating pain, I pleaded with Jeannie, "What's taking so long?"

I'll always remember her answer. "God's in control here," she said. "His timing is perfect."

Suddenly two nurses in graying white uniforms began rolling me down a corridor. Parked gurneys and well-worn chairs became obstacles as we zigzagged down the hall. A short, stocky orthopedic surgeon examined me. As he barked commands, nurses scurried around me like hummingbirds. Soon an old, portable x-ray machine appeared next to my gurney.

A burly nurse tried to take my shirt off. She straightened my arm and as she lifted my shoulder I screamed in anguish, "Cut it off! **Cut it off!**" After much hesitation she found a pair of scissors and cut the shirt from my tormented body. Much later I learned of the value some Colombians place on clothing. Although just a work shirt to me, it was a choice garment to my benefactor.

They began taking x-rays. I could see the equipment was quite old, but at the time it hardly mattered. My attention was riveted on the painful process of placing x-ray film under my back. Time after time I endured this modern form of medieval torture. Then my Colombian doctor smiled broadly as he announced that I had no broken bones.

Even with such good news I couldn't smile. The prognosis was short-lived anyway, as Dr. Brabon, with a far more prudent evaluation, said, "We've got to be certain." "We'll take more x-rays tomorrow with the permanent equipment."

Engulfed in another flare of pain, I knew the correct diagnosis had eluded them.

They rolled me to a mint green room containing a single bed four inches higher than my gurney. Three slightly built nurses attempted to transfer me to the bed, but only succeeded in dropping me halfway through the move. Ila suffered with me when I came down on the uneven surfaces.

With a mind confused by trauma, I wondered how Christ's love could be defended in the face of my suffering and the possibility of total paralysis. Particularly since I was joyously serving Him at the moment I was struck down. Would the God to whom I had given my life purposefully counter with such a wounding thrust? Or was this Satan's ultimate challenge in my life? My spirits sank. How could this be happening to me?

It's only human to wonder, I suppose. After all, who doesn't? Fortunately God neutralized these thoughts by allowing me to feel His presence. It was the same feeling I experienced immediately after falling, when in total agony I prayed for Jesus' help. Now, as then, I was rescued by the Holy Spirit and my fears vanished.

A single pain shot, one of two I would receive during my five days in Colombia, helped me through the first night. Ila tried to rest on a flimsy leather settee which converted to a mini-bed. But sleep was impossible. Caught in an unlikely drama and filled with anxiety, we faced an undeniable truth. We were in very serious trouble. As we prayed intently for

Christ's intervention, I continued to receive the quieting assurance of the Holy Spirit. Even in the silence and darkness of that first night, I knew no fear.

Tuesday brought the second and last pain shot--and a lot of visitors from the seminary. It also brought a number of complete strangers to our door, surreptitiously peeking in to see this Christian "gringo". News of the "rich" American who had broken his back working on a church was spreading fast. "Had God already begun to use me?" I wondered.

There was plenty of activity that Tuesday, but no x-rays. When my doctor arrived late that afternoon, I told him of this incredible situation. Unruffled, he told me in heavily accented English that the staff had been too busy to get to me, but I would be x-rayed "first thing tomorrow".

Our situation during the second night improved very little. We were able to snatch a few disjointed segments of sleep, but it was due to exhaustion rather than contentment. On Wednesday morning the nurses moved me from my bed to a gurney and then by elevator to the x-ray department. The moment we arrived the attendants hurriedly dismissed us, and I was expeditiously returned to my room.

Ila's expression mirrored her disbelief. "No x-rays?" she asked in a voice choked with emotion. Once more I was transferred from gurney to bed. Gloom and foreboding flourished proportionately with time and pain.

Later, through an interpreter, we were told that the Marxist guerrilla group known as M-19 had blown up a water line that serviced the hospital. The nurses were unable to develop x-rays without water. This made me think of M-19's involvement with the Medellin drug cartel. M-19 had taken over the Colombian Palace of Justice (Supreme Court) and assassinated eleven justices in 1985, all because the justices were considering a law allowing indicted drug lords to be extradited to the U.S. to stand trial.

Early that evening the water line was repaired and my x-rays finally taken. I'll never forget the doctor's words when he viewed them; "Oh my, we have a problem here! You have a serious burst fracture in your spine. We've got to get a CAT scan immediately."

My heart sank. The room seemed to become smaller and my attention was distracted. Oblivious to my mental state, he droned on: "We've got to be very careful when we move you." Then gesturing, as if breaking an imaginary twig, he continued. "A twist, a bend, anything could sever your spinal cord and you would never walk again."

That evening when the missionaries and crusaders brought our daily ration of drinking water, we again prayed for Jesus' help. The doctor needed better x-rays for medical reasons, and we needed reassurance that "in the end" it would all turn out okay. In spite of the many unanswered questions, I felt no fear of the unknown. The Holy Spirit whispered, "Cast all your anxiety on Him because He cares for you."

Now that we had a diagnosis, telephone calls were made to MFM in Greenwood. The OMS and MFM prayer chains went into immediate action. It wasn't until much later that I learned of the magnitude of this intercession. It was truly uplifting to think that Christians all over the world--from Canada to Australia--were praying for *me*, a person they never heard of.

On Thursday morning I was taken by ambulance to another hospital for a CAT scan. The ambulance was just an empty van and its driver had no medical knowledge, but we arrived safely. I was moved a lot on this trip--from bed to gurney to a stretcher to the x-ray table and back again--but the Lord protected me from further injury.

That afternoon after a solemn greeting, my doctor read from a worn notebook. I had suffered a spinal burst fracture at L3, and multiple bone fragments had been spotted in the spinal canal. That wasn't all. The space through which my spinal cord ran was reduced sixty percent, and the surrounding edges were jagged. The impending danger to my spinal cord was uppermost in his mind, and it was reflected in his tone and mannerisms. He recommended immediate surgery.

Ila and Jeannie were there when the news broke. Following an awkward silence they tried to be positive. But the prognosis was staggering--especially when the doctor could not assure us the sixty percent reduction could be corrected. He then estimated my return to the U.S. at six months or more, and went so far as to say I would be better off not to have the surgery in Colombia. How I could return to the States in this condition, however, was beyond his comprehension. For a few moments we were overcome by this collision with reality.

That evening the missionaries and crusaders held a prayer meeting in my room.

Friday dawned with no solution at hand. A phone call to Avianca, the major Colombian airline, merely revealed that their policies prevented transporting stretcher patients. Due to the unavailability of a local air-ambulance service, it would be impossible for me to go any other way.

As the day wore on we continued praying that the Lord, in His power, would provide a miracle. Then missionaries from the seminary arrived. Led by Margaret Brabon, the OMS field leader, they circled my bed and went to prayer, asking for both compassion and wisdom.

Two hours after they left, the jangling phone awakened me from a restless sleep. Avianca had relented; they would take me on tomorrow's flight to Miami. Praise God! We were absolutely jubilant. The Lord had indeed worked another miracle. Later we learned that Margaret Brabon had called a retired Avianca official, a personal friend, who interceded on my behalf. We couldn't have been more grateful.

My doctor came that evening and was astonished at the news. He gave orders for my release. I remember thanking him, and as I did, handing him a New Testament. "You know," I assured him, "it was the Lord who opened these doors."

After a restless night, Saturday morning finally arrived. We were to leave the hospital at six a.m., but we were ready at five. Surprisingly, my doctor walked in the room. I certainly didn't expect to see him that early. We exchanged pleasantries and he wished us good luck. As he was leaving the room, however, he dropped another bomb. "By the way," he said, "your left heel is crushed and will also need surgery. You haven't been moving it, and the pain in your back has masked it, but it's in bad shape. You might want to have them look at that, too."

We were finally on our way to the airport--a two-hour ride up the mountain. There was a short delay while they checked my status with Avianca, then the ambulance pulled onto the tarmac. Dave Cosby spoke to the pilot and stewardess. It was decided that any attempt to carry my stretcher up the steep stairway to the plane's door would be too dangerous. Another solution was necessary.

As they pondered the problem, Jeannie informed the captain of my condition. Her instructions went beyond a simple medical report, however. Jeannie let him know that he was to treat me as "precious cargo" and fly the plane very carefully.

Jeannie then discovered that the stretcher we were counting on was a swayback piece of cloth--something like a hammock.

"It'll never do!" she insisted. "Unless a board is located, he can't leave!"

We went to prayer! By now we were also attracting a small crowd, even though we were on the tarmac a quarter of a mile from the terminal.

Ron and Dave immediately went in search of a board. Walking away from the terminal, they approached a fenced area where guards stood on duty. As soon as they told the guards our predicament, they handed them a board of perfect proportions. Miracle number--sorry, I've lost count.

Then I saw a forklift approaching. "Hate to tell you this," said Dave, "but we're going to lift you up to the side door on this forklift. Can you handle it?" Ila and I looked at each other. "Let's do it," I said.

They placed me on a pallet held by the forklift's tongs while Ron and Dave steadied me. I heard the roar of the diesel engine, smelled black oily exhaust, and felt chains engage as we started up. Wobbling, ever more upward, the pallet shook relentlessly. Looking up past Ron's and Dave's worried expressions, I saw blue sky and white, puffy clouds. The wind sliced under my bedsheet as we inched closer to the plane's door.

Since I was parallel with the plane, I had to be twisted in order to go through the doorway. Under great stress and moving carefully on the wobbly pallet, Dave and Ron slowly rotated my stretcher until those on the plane could grab one end and pull me to safety. Relieved, I lay on the aircraft floor looking up into the faces of pilots, stewardesses, missionaries, and passengers. They were all talking at once. But I made it. I was on board!

They pushed three seatbacks forward and placed my stretcher on the makeshift platform. Ila sat next to me all the way to Miami, holding me, boosting my spirits. When we arrived, paramedics met us and spent 30 minutes immobilizing me. I was taken off in the same manner, but instead of a forklift, they used a Dobbs food-catering truck. All this, and no fear.

MFM, working with a Christian friend, Captain John Hill of the Indiana State Police, had made arrangements for the ambulance, a hospital, and a surgeon. It felt good to be back in the American medical system. I was immediately placed in a "roto-bed", which slowly rotated to prevent the formation of blood clots, while a series of doctors examined me.

All was not rosy, however. A medical strike was in progress, and my hospital was the only one in Miami accepting trauma cases. I would have to wait six more days for surgery. Two dear ladies from our church in Greenwood, Indiana--Carole Leedy and Margie Puckett--flew to Miami at their own expense to bolster Ila. They stayed with her for over a week. Roy and Carolyn McCook, Marian Giles, and Geneva DeYoung--all OMS missionaries working in Miami's ethnic neighborhoods--visited me daily.

During that waiting period, my chief surgeon walked in, studying my x-rays. After discovering I had been working for the Lord on a missionary work crusade, he bluntly said, "You must be worshiping the wrong God."

I wasn't very alert at that point and didn't respond. He turned away. But before he got to the door he stopped and said, "You know, on second thought, considering the nature of your injuries and the fact that you weren't killed or paralyzed, I believe you're worshiping the right God after all."

All I could say was one word, "Amen!"

Eleven days after the fall I had surgery. With so many people praying, I sensed no fear as I entered that operating room. Guided by God's hands, the surgeons did an excellent job of putting six screws in my heel and two six-inch steel rods in my back. Using bone from my pelvis, they covered the rods.

When I came back to my room 12 hours later, I felt about as bad as a guy can feel. It surely wasn't a "Sunday on the farm." But, spiritually I was on top of the world. Jesus had brought me through the valley.

Surprisingly, however, the rough part wasn't over. Eight days later a blood clot hit my lungs. The pain was severe and a shot of morphine didn't faze it. I was rapidly getting to the point that I couldn't breathe. Once again I thought I was going to die. Without fear, I remember praying, "Jesus, just one more breath." Again, He was faithful. He brought me through the valley a second time.

Ila was at my bedside every minute of this ordeal. Thirty days after surgery we flew home by air-ambulance. Warren and Velma Hardig of MFM, Pastor Charles Lake of the Community Church of Greenwood, and my friend Bob Poppleton met us at the airport. When I was settled back in my own bed once again, we held hands and gave unbridled thanks to the Lord for my rescue. That was, undoubtedly, one of the happiest days of my life.

I was in a wheelchair for three months, on anti-coagulants for six months, and in a backbrace for over a year. It gave me plenty of time to think about my life.

I realized that Jesus had saved me in two ways--spiritually and physically. He did this, even after I ignored Him for the better part of my life. I was most undeserving, and I knew it. I was rediscovering God's grace and power as an active participant in His grand plan. Just being aware of this was overwhelming. Realizing how magnificent and holy God is made me feel very, very small. How could I not have seen this before? Now it was so clear that Satan had blinded me with his small gods--like man's recognition and worldly gain.

Initially I saw this tragedy in the same way as a nail might look at a hammer. Everything was beating me down. I was struck time after time with different medical problems and an ample amount of pain. But because of my faith in God through Jesus Christ, I saw who was holding the hammer. God used this crisis (He didn't cause it) to teach me many things I needed to know about Him, and to prepare me for a new life of usefulness for Him. My path seemed very clear: Full-time surrender and full-time service. I joined OMS as a missionary in January of 1988 and am currently the Men For Missions International Administrator. One of my duties involves writing for and editing the MFM *Action* magazine. Through this opportunity I am now speaking for Jesus--encouraging men in every walk of life to release their personal skills and abilities in practical, direct missionary involvement.

Today the steel in my body is nothing more than a gentle reminder of His mercy. Through His resplendent grace He has been faithful to a sinner. He continues to mold me-- conforming me to the likeness of His Son. To Him I owe everything. To Him I give everything.

Epilogue

People and events have the potential to influence our attitudes and beliefs. It is important, therefore, that among such persuasive forces we have the ability to distinguish good from evil. To possess that ability we must adopt the bedrock standards of Scripture.

Without such guidelines, we resist life-sharpening processes--primarily because they attack our ego. We choose to ignore them, but in doing so, we will pay the consequences. The Bible provides an example as it tells the story of the rich man and Lazarus.

The rich man dressed in purple and fine linen, would not stoop to help Lazarus, the beggar covered with sores. His self-importance dominated his compassion, thereby preventing Lazarus' plight (a life-sharpening situation) from influencing him.

Compassion finally came--but it was too late. Luke uses graphic language as he describes the rich man's plea: "Then I beg you, father, send Lazarus to my father's house, for I have five brothers. Let him warn them, so that they will not also come to this place of torment" (Luke 16:27 NIV).

From this verse comes the allegory, "Everyone in hell has the heart of an evangelist". But what about those of us on earth? Statistics tell us that 95% of those who claim to be a Christian have never led a lost soul to Christ.

If only more people would restrain their egotism and become sensitive to the priceless lessons taught by life-sharpening people.

"But how?" you ask.

If we live our lives by faithfully serving Jesus Christ, Scripture will become the basis of our principles and behavior. As we grow in His Word, we will improve our ability to screen out negative influences and incorporate those of value. This capacity will increase our sensitivity to life-sharpening events--even when their occurrence is not apparent.

Such was the case when I attended my first MFM banquet. I didn't consider Harry Burr a life-sharpening individual at the time, but the effect of his words *was* life-changing. Nor did I consider the possibility that God might use an insignificant beggar in Haiti to spur me to become a missionary. But God did!

All of the men in this book have sharpened my life, as well. Some in a bold, adventurous manner, others in a more undefined, subtle way. Nevertheless, the effect has been the same. When I became a Christian I surrendered my ego. In doing so, I began to develop sensitivity to the wisdom around me. I began to see what I could not see; to hear what I could not hear. And from this valuable insight grew compassion--a tenderness of heart which focused on the lost.

I've learned that millions die each year, only to join the rich man in hell. In India alone 600,000 cities and villages are without an evangelical witness. Less than one percent of Japan's population is Christian. What of the millions in China? Africa? Consider the millions in our own land.

I also discovered that an abundance of resources exists to correct these problems. In fact, it's all around us, just waiting to be energized. It's laymen. I encourage the church to place more significance on the compelling need of the lost, and through vigorous evangelical principles activate its laymen. Without that, it will never reach the multitudes.

Dr. Ferguson, the founder of Men For Missions International, declared: "If we take men to the mission field, the sight of millions bound in spiritual darkness will spark the compassion they now suppress in their hearts. They'll return with the fire of the Holy Spirit, ready to roll up their sleeves and participate in the harvest."

The men portrayed in this book possess that compassion and fire. Although manifested in different ways, its basis lies in the Bible, it's polished through fellowship, and it benefits the lost--those for whom Jesus Christ died.

They are humble men. They are often ignored--sometimes even belittled by those who have adopted secular standards. But their relationship with our Creator, and the life He lives through them, allows me to evaluate them with a different measure. When I do, they become *great* men. I will continually thank God for the privilege of meeting them, and the sharpening effect they have had on my life.

I will also go to heaven deeply indebted to Mr. Ralph Watts of Houston, Texas, and Mr. Stanley Tam of Lima, Ohio. They, too, present a witness framed and colored by boldness. I stand before them a fledgling student--awestruck by their capacity to petition God for the accomplishment of His will. When I am weak and in doubt, I find strength and wisdom in their examples.

Now you have read about solid Christians who live for Christ every day. But just ten?   No, they represent thousands of other MFMers across the world who have pledged:

> I will do whatever God asks me to do,
> I will go wherever Gods asks me to go, and
> I will give whatever God asks me to give.

But what about you?   Would you take that pledge?   It would be wise to ask yourself this very important question.

Are you a Christian?

Some people believe they are Christian because they aren't something else, like a Moslem, a Hindu, or an atheist. Some believe they are Christian because their parents were, or because they live in a "Christian" nation. And most sadly, some believe they are Christians because they go to church and think of themselves as "nice guys".

Nice guys are people who never commit crimes or misdemeanors. They're polite, have high morals, and don't lie, cheat, or steal. But being a law-abiding, compassionate, church-goer is the *result* of being a Christian, it's not your ticket to heaven.

How then? First you must understand that [God] "is not willing that any should perish, but that all should come to repentance" (II Peter 3:9). What is repentance? It's the acknowledgement and confession of your past sins, *and* a heartfelt desire to stop sinning.

I John 1:9 says, "If we confess our sins, He is faithful and just to forgive us our sins and to cleanse us from all unrighteousness."

However, you must also believe. Romans 10:9-10 says, "That if you confess with your mouth, 'Jesus is Lord,' and believe in your heart that God raised him from the dead, you will be saved. For it is with your heart that you believe and are justified, and it is with your mouth that you confess and are saved."

Finally, Jesus himself said in John 14:6, "I am the way and the truth and the life. No one comes to the Father except through me."

If you are uncertain about your salvation, now is the time to resolve those doubts once and for all. Simply ask Jesus for the forgiveness of your sins, and invite Him into your heart. Ask Him to live His life in you. Romans 6:11 tells us, "...count yourselves dead to sin but alive to God in Christ Jesus."

If you are sincere and really want to follow Him to heaven, pray this prayer:

O God, I confess that I have sinned against You. I am sorry for those sins. I now want to turn away from my sinful life. I openly receive Christ as my Savior. I gratefully acknowledge that He died for my sins. At this time I make Him my Lord. From this moment on I will serve Him. In Jesus' name I pray.

Now continue seeking Him in prayer. You may have complete confidence that God's guiding presence will point you in the direction of His will. The important thing is to grow. Read the Bible, attend church, and fellowship with other Christians, for Proverbs 27:17 tells us:

"As iron sharpens iron, so one man sharpens another."

Glossary of Terms

Action Magazine:

A quarterly publication of Men For Missions International. A free subscription can be obtained by writing MFMI, P.O. Box A, Greenwood, IN 46142.

Associate Staff:

Laymen who are neither lay missionaries nor employees of OMS. They volunteer their services and are not included in regular missionary benefits. They are appointed by the MFMI cabinet for two-year terms.

Cabinet:

Made up of men representing all parts of the United States, the Cabinet establishes policy and gives direction to MFMI. There is also an international cabinet.

Council: A regional group of laymen and pastors who meet monthly to assist the work of MFMI through prayer, raising funds to provide financial support, conducting retreats and banquets, and sending council members on crusades.

Crusade: A group of laymen and/or pastors who travel to an OMS mission field or center under the auspices of MFMI. Paying their own way, participants go during vacation time. There are four types of crusades listed in this glossary.

Crusade Director: A member of the MFMI staff who directs crusades.

Evangelism Crusade: The evangelism crusade is tailored for people who want to participate in impact witnessing on the mission field. With teammates and an interpreter, participants conduct door-to-door witness campaigns, evening rallies, and follow-up ministries.

Men For Missions International:

The Laymen's Voice of OMS International. Through MFMI thousands of men from multiple church affiliations and every walk of life have found a channel for harnessing and releasing personal skills and abilities in practical, direct missionary involvement. No dues are required, and membership is open to any man who pledges: I will do whatever God asks me to do; I will go wherever God asks me to go; I will give whatever God asks me to give.

MFMI:

Men For Missions International, P.O. Box A, Greenwood, IN 46142, 317/881-6752. The initials are often shortened to MFM.

Missionary Support:

OMS International is a Christian faith mission supported by the voluntary contributions of God's people. Missionaries are responsible for generating contributions to OMS sufficient to cover expenses attributable to their ministry (see "shares" in this glossary.)

OMS International:

OMS International is a faith mission which stands in the historic evangelical tradition of the church. In response to the Great Commission, OMS emphasizes evangelism, training of national leadership for ministry, and church planting. Copies of OMS Articles of Faith are available by writing OMS International, P.O. Box A, Greenwood, IN 46142.

Professional Services Program:

The specialized training of medical, dental, and other professional people, is a valuable resource for missions. Some offer their services without charge, while others assist where needed both through their skills and as a witness to their counterparts overseas.

Regional Directors:

MFMI regional directors assist the national director by implementing and supervising the activities of MFMI within their geographic areas.

Shares:

Gifts to OMS for the support of individual missionaries or projects. Usually given in multiples of $20, they are considered a faith prom- ise--a spiritual covenant between the giver and God. As He provides, the giver contributes. (See missionary support in this glossary).

Special Crusade:

Different from a regular work, witness, or evangelism crusade, a special crusade involves dedications, anniversaries, Caribbean cruises, Orient tours, etc. Offered only on special occasions, they are not part of the regular crusade schedule.

Trucking For Missions
Program:

Under the direction of a coordina- tor, volunteer drivers using loaned vehicles or the MFMI truck, haul hundreds of tons of mission equipment to ports of export each year. They also move missionary freight within the country.

Wings For Missions: Under the direction of a coordinator, Christian pilots assist OMS by transporting missionary personnel or supplies. A pilot may fly himself or lend his plane for mission use.

Witness Crusade: Witness crusades provide opportunity to see missions in action. Crusaders view a broad spectrum of mission work, as well as share a witness with those of another culture.

Work Crusade: Work Crusades consist of MFMers with able bodies and willing hands. They build or repair missionary homes, churches, clinics, or schools. Teams go, usually for two weeks, and donate their technical skills and abilities.

May I Help?

If you have decided to make a commitment to Christ and are searching for answers, I can be of assistance by providing you with Christian literature based on biblical truths.

Don't delay. Your reconciliation with Christ is the most important thing you have to do today--or in this lifetime. Write me at P.O. Box A, Greenwood, Indiana, 46142.

Warren Hardig